Are we Doomed to Secular Stagnation?

Uwe Petersen

Are we Doomed to Secular Stagnation?

Limitations of Supply-Side Economic Policies

Original German Title:
Säkulare Stagnation unser Schicksal?
Grenzen der angebotsorientierten Wirtschaftspolitik
Published 2014

Translated by: Word Converters Limited

Published 2014

Book cover design:
Tom Jay - www.tomjay.de
Photo: © Tijana - fotolia.com

ISBN -13: 978-1503319103

ISBN-10:1503319105

www.philosope.de
Dr. Uwe Petersen
Dubrowstraße 49, 14129 Berlin
Tel.: +49308014369, Email: philosope@arcor.de

Contents

Introduction 9
A. Secular stagnation and its manifestations 12
I. What is secular stagnation? 12
1. Traditional secular stagnation 13
2. What caused the traditionally stagnating economic order to give way to a growth economy? 14
3. Capitalist secular stagnation 15
3.1 Ever-increasing discrepancy between economic savings and profitable economic investment opportunities. 17
3.2 How are surplus economic savings possible in relation to stagnating investment opportunities? 23
3.3 The tendency for rationalisation investments to outweigh consumer goods innovations and expansion 24
3.4 Ways of compensating for the demand gap in a national economy through wage increases, state spending, increasing consumer debt, capital exports and burning capital. 25
3.4.1 Ways of compensating for the demand gap in a national economy through wage increase 25
3.4.2. Ways of compensating for the demand gap in a national economy through state spending 27
3.4.4 Ways of compensating for the demand gap in a national economy by burning capital 33

II. Stages of secular stagnation since the 1960s and the economic measures taken to combat its symptoms whilst simultaneously increasing the fragility of the economic system 36
1. The beginnings of modern secular stagnation following the end of the postwar reconstruction period 36
2. Stagflation 39
3. The end of the inflation within stagflation through deindustrialisation 41
4. The financialisation of the economy, and how it has degenerated into a casino 49

III. The economic development of Japan as a model case of capitalist secular stagnation 53

B. Why is the present capitalist secular stagnation not recognised by prevailing neoclassical economic theory? 62
I. Individualistic ideology 63
II. Inadequate theory of the development of the relationship between economic supply and economic demand 65
III. Lack of understanding of the role of money in a primarily capital-market-oriented economy 73
IV. Inadequate theory of economic growth 83
1. Only seeming growth, once the impact on economic growth of costs for the protection of resources and the reparation of environmental damage are taken into account 86
2. False equation of economic growth with the improvement of general prosperity 87
3. The problematic equation of economic growth with improvements in general prosperity over the course of globalisation 96
3.1 Insufficient attention to the detrimental impact on general prosperity of the distribution of technical and economic know-how in the course of globalisation 97
3.2 Insufficient attention to the detrimental impact on general prosperity of the narrow concentration of private economic power and its unequal distribution in the course of globalisation 103
C. The need for a new understanding of the principles of a healthy economy and economic policy measures to combat secular stagnation and stabilise the economy 112
I. Improving market opportunities for all citizens by overcoming the entrenched practice of feudal inheritance which is incompatible with the system 117
II. The need to implement economic policy to align economic savings with real economic investment opportunities in order to overcome secular stagnation 120
III. The 're-naturalisation' of the money and capital markets 122
1. The neutralisation of circulating government bonds in order to educe currency speculation instead of acquisition by central banks 122
2. Banking regulation 127
3. Regulation of the money market 129
IV. Limitations of globalisation 132
1. Reducing export and import surpluses 135
2. Better assignment of profit to operating facilities to ensure appropriate taxation 136
3. Empowering employees in order to protect jobs 138

4. More state investment to fund collective needs and to prevent
the unnecessary relocation of operations 139
**D. Criteria of secular stagnation and necessary
economic policy measures** 141
I. Criterion: Higher savings than there are lucrative private sector
investment opportunities in the real economy 141
II. Criterion: extreme inequality in the distribution of income and wealth 142
III. Criterion: very low interest rates 142
IV. Rising property prices due to increasing pressure to invest 143
V. Criterion: uneven balance of foreign trade 144
**E. How economic policy is still only treating the economy's symptoms
and this is increasing its susceptibility to crises, as illustrated by the
Merkel government** 147
I. How the Merkel government's economic and taxation policies
are not reducing export surpluses and are thereby increasing the
economy's susceptibility to crises 148
II. How the German social security system encourages secular stagnation 152
III. How the Merkel government is exacerbating secular stagnation
through insufficient public investment 154
V. Insufficient reduction of public debt in order to lessen the economy's
susceptibility to crises caused by speculation, and in order to act as
a role model for other Eurozone counties 156
VI. The Merkel government's lack of understanding of monetary policy
in times of secular stagnation 160
Conclusion 162
Biblography 165
Author 171

Introduction

On 21 November 2013, K. Singer wrote: 'Larry Summers, [¹] during a speech at the IMF's annual research conference last week, stirred up a hornet's nest by painting a picture of a future with chronically weak demand and sluggish economic growth: a phenomenon known as 'secular stagnation'.

He is not the first to point to such a scenario. Paul Krugman picked up on the 'secular stagnation' hypothesis from the early postwar period in his blog two years ago. He credits Summers with having done an excellent job of reviving this hypothesis.'[2] And George Soros, one of the best-known hedge fund managers in the world, who forced the British government to pull the pound from the European Exchange Rate Mechanism, says: 'The Euro crisis is now comparable with the Great Depression of the 1930s. Europe has reached a nadir and faces a long period of stagnation.'[3]

---

[1] From 1995 to 1999 Larry Summers was deputy to the Treasury Secretary Robert Rubin, before becoming Secretary of the Treasury himself inBill Clinton's cabinet from 1999 to 2001. During this period, Summers supported the deregulation of the financial markets effected by the Gramm–Leach–Bliley Act of 1999, which largely abolished the segregation of commercial and investment banking. The deregulation of over-the-counter derivatives was later seen as one of the main causes of the financial crisis in 2007. In hindsight, Clinton regretted having listened to Rubin's and Summers' advice. In 2008, Summers was appointed to the post of Director of the National Economic Council by US President-elect Barack Obama. At the end of 2010 he left the National Economic Council; it was claimed that he would otherwise have had to forfeit his permanent position as a university professor. He returned to Harvard University. This summer, Summers emerged as a leading candidate to succeed Bernanke as Head of the Federal Reserve. He ultimately withdrew his candidacy following opposition from liberal Democrats in the US Senate, leaving the way clear for Yellen.
Source: http://www.timepatternanalysis.de/Blog/2013/11/21/summers-sakulare-stagnation/
[2] Source: loc. cit.
[3] Carsten Brönstrup interviews George Soros: 'Europe faces a long period of stagnation'

'The weak development of prices in the Eurozone gives cause for concern in terms of potential deflation. The markets' short-term and medium-term inflation expectations, which have fallen even lower in recent months, and forecasts by the ECB, all point to a long period of very low rates of inflation lying well below the ECB's target. 'The danger of a self-perpetuating deflationary spiral in the event of continuing low interest rates is very real," say Kerstin Bernoth, Marcel Fratzscher and Philipp König from the German Institute for Economic Research (DIW Berlin).[4]

Christian Reiermann and Anne Seith report: 'At his press conference at the close of the Spring Meeting of the IMF and the World Bank, which focused on international currency, Draghi almost let slip a telltale word. "Defla..." began the Italian, only to catch himself and substitute 'low inflation' in its place. The word Draghi dared not utter, however, was already all over Washington. Deflation - that phenomenon of steadily falling prices which is currently striking fear into the hearts of those in charge of central banks and ministries the world over.'[5]

On 5 June 2014, the European Central Bank stepped up its fight against the threat of deflation. *Tagesschau.de* reports: 'The European Central Bank (ECB) is dropping its interest rates to record lows. The key interest rate is being cut from 0.25 to 0.15%, the Central Bank announced. In future, banks will also have to pay a penalty interest rate when they park money with the ECB. The deposit rate is being cut below zero for the first time, to minus 0.10%.

The intention is to force financial institutions to make funds available to businesses in the form of loans. The low interest rate is intended to boost investment and consumption.

The ECB also announced that it wanted to boost lending, in southern European countries in particular, through cash injections worth billions of Euros. The Central Bank will continue to lend

---

Star investor George Soros on Angela Merkel's management of the crisis and the possible breakdown of the European Union, in: *Der Tagespiegel* No. 21970, 26/2/2014, p.12.
[4] DIW press release on 19/03/2014: *The risk of deflation in the Eurozone.*
5 Christian Reiermann and Anne Seith: *Währungen Die letzte Waffe [Currencies, The Last Weapon]*, in: *Der Spiegel* No.17, 19/4/14, p. 60.

money at favourable terms, said ECB President Mario Draghi, and will offer, for the first time, loans with four-year terms lasting until 2018. Unlike previous longer-term loans, these ones come with strings attached; commercial banks will have to prove that they are passing on funds at least in part to companies and private customers. It is hoped that this will stimulate economic activity. The programme will initially have a maximum available volume of 400 billion Euros.

At the peak of the financial crisis, in late 2011 and early 2012, the ECB had already flooded the financial system with two liquidity injections of at least 500 billion Euros each. At that time, however, the banks had invested a large part of the money in government bonds, seen as safe investments - which may have propped up states and banks, but did not lead to any new loans.

The ECB's decisions have been prompted by the fact that inflation rates are so low, at less than one percent, and by the still-sluggish economic situation in the Eurozone. The ECB's target is a 2% inflation rate. The actual figure, however, has failed to meet this target for months now. This has given rise to fears of deflation - in other words, a downward spiral in prices.'[6]

What is secular stagnation and how can it be identified?

---

[6] *Kampf gegen Deflation. Leitzins nahe Null, Strafzins für Banken [The Fight Against Deflation: Key Interest Rate Close to Zero, Penalty Interest Rate for Banks]*
http://www.tagesschau.de/wirtschaft/ezb-leitzins-100.html

A. Secular stagnation and its manifestations

I. What is secular stagnation?

An economy can be viewed as social behaviour involving the division of labour in order to satisfy people's needs. Its aim and purpose, then, are to satisfy society's needs in an optimal way. Needless to say, the optimal satisfaction of needs is dependent upon generally limited natural resources, the conditions of production and societal power relations. These factors too are interdependent. Undeveloped forces of production lead to a situation in which the few oppress the many, and in some cases turn the many into slaves, in order to live as comfortably as possible themselves. Under such conditions of production, even in earlier eras, the only possible development was a cultural one. This required people to be freed up to create cultural assets, and the masses had to work together for the few.

With the development of the methods of production within a given need structure, the pressure on the working masses can naturally be eased, and this is the case particularly when economic progress is dependent upon the intelligence and skill of the creators. This was how the developing bourgeoisie was able to end the rule of the aristocracy.

Karl Marx predicted that another consequence of the development of the forces of production would be that the rule of the bourgeoisie would be overthrown in a proletarian revolution and that then, thanks to the developed forces of production, each would be able to live according to his own needs.

Marx, however, was labouring under the illusion that
- work is a basic human need, and that all human beings would contribute willingly, according to their abilities, to ensure the provision of the necessary products and services;
- that production and distribution did not require ordered and hierarchical structures and could be organised by democratic councils; and
- that needs could not be multiplied and diversified by new products, leading to a never-ending conflict over the distribution of resources.

In effect, therefore, Karl Marx had a stationary understanding of economics. According to this understanding, a stationary, primitive communist society is supposed to develop into a class-based society, which develops its productive forces in order to then be resurrected as a classless society.

Liberal economic theorists do not share this view of capitalism. They believe that the Industrial Revolution was the beginning of permanent economic growth. This is why liberal economic theory, which dominates the economic debate to this day, views economic stagnation as a disease. But industrial nations, as will be shown, have been suffering from secular stagnation since at least the 1960s, i.e. the end of the postwar period of reconstruction. We must therefore distinguish between *traditional* secular stagnation and *capitalist* secular stagnation.

1. Traditional secular stagnation

Secular stagnation was the normal state of national economies until the Industrial Revolution. Under the prevailing conditions of production, people produced whatever it was possible to produce. Production methods remained the same for many centuries and even millennia; in other words, innovation took place only over long periods of time.

Wikipedia states: 'Across the world, the Stone Age is the earliest epoch in human history, and is characterised by the dominant tradition of stone tools. It began (as far as we know) with the oldest tools ever found, dating back to around 2.6 million years ago in Africa, and is there referred to as the Early Stone Age.[1] ... The end of the stone age, with the emergence of the material copper, ushered in a new epoch - the Copper Age - which varied from region to region. In some parts of the world, it was not until the Early Bronze Age that the Stone Age gave way to a new era. In central Europe this happened around 2200 BC.'[7]

'At the end of the Stone Age a transition period began, during which people started to work with a radically different material: metal. New and better characteristics meant that this material could be put to previously unknown uses, but also called for much more

---

[7] http://de.wikipedia.org/wiki/Steinzeit

complex handling and technology, as well as a functioning system of long distance trade to give people access to the sought-after material, which was not available everywhere. This transitional phase is called the Copper Age, also known as the Chalcolithic or Eneolithic Age. It came to an end with the beginning of the Bronze Age.'[8]

This was followed by the Iron Age beginning around 1200 B.C., which lasted, to all intents and purposes, until the start of the Industrial Revolution. Until that time, new and more refined manual skills developed only over long periods of time.

Traditional societies could be very productive, creating sophisticated cultural assets and waging wars. Each society produced only as much as it needed. This led to disparities in income. Slaves and people from the lower classes were forced to supply all the necessary goods and services that were not obtained as the spoils of war through the invasion and plunder of other countries. Because the methods of production did not change, the only way of growing the economy was to squeeze more and more out of slaves or subjects. True economic growth, which is synonymous with an increase in general prosperity, is only possible through inventions and investment.

2. What caused the traditionally stagnating economic order to give way to a growth economy?

The prerequisites for a developing, growing economy were science and technological progress, as well as a civilisation which could support economic development.

The intellectual orientation of the old advanced civilisations, however, was backward-looking, focused on past eras which people tended to view as 'golden ages'. In East Asian cultures with their cults of ancestor worship, people looked to the lives and knowledge of forefathers and mythical sages for guidance. In India, the material world was seen as a world of illusion, *Maya*. Desires and actions in this world of illusion were thought to bind the soul and generate karmic obligations, forcing souls into new incarnations over and over again. The Indians therefore attempted to break this bond between their souls and the external world and to

---

[8] Loc. cit.

enter Nirvana. Muslims, who had played an important role in defining European spiritual development in its origins - as evidenced by the sophisticated Arabian culture in Moorish Spain - were trapped by their fixation on their otherworldly god, who was seen as the sole source of all creativity. Economic conditions remained at the same stage of development, in a state of *secular stagnation*.

Only in Europe did Greek thought and Jewish world orientation develop into science and technology, and religious eschatology into an ideology of progress. This was what gave rise to Europe's technological revolution, which has been driving forward development ever since, and to what is commonly known as *economic growth*.

According to the ideal of progress characterised by the self-determining, self-developing individual, every person is supposed to be the architect of his or her own good fortune or misfortune, to earn a living through work or investment and also, if possible, to accumulate wealth. It was thought that the market would guarantee that individuals would produce and sell what was of the greatest benefit to society as a whole. Competition between suppliers of goods and work was supposed to ensure that these suppliers were obliged to sell as cheaply as possible, since it was only those offering the cheapest goods who would prove successful.

In economic terms, *technological progress* became associated with the bourgeoisie's *profit interest*, and thus, in their hands, led to the creation of economic prosperity and the liberation of the bourgeoisie from the rule of the aristocracy.

3. Capitalist secular stagnation

A national economy is balanced when demand matches economic supply. This does not mean that all products and services can be sold and/or that they can command the desired price. If the prices of certain products fall, or if they are not being sold at all, unused purchasing power must be expended in larger amounts on other products, which then rise in price. Such price shifts are desirable in the market economy, because they help suppliers learn from experience by adjusting their supply to match demand more and more closely, or by improving their production.

Overall, however, total demand must equal the total of goods and services supplied; because incomes emerge as *requirements* in the course of the production process. If incomes are not spent then goods remain unsold; production is restricted accordingly and the economy stagnates, and may even fall into a depression.

When there is less economic demand than supply, purchasing power is only saved and not invested. The progressive tendency for savings to outweigh investment opportunities in the real economy is thus the main cause of *capitalist secular stagnation*.

Another cause is the progressive tendency for rationalisation investments to outweigh investment in innovation and expansion. This leads to more workers being laid off than there are new jobs being created.

Naturally, since those in lower income brackets save less than those on higher incomes, less savings are made in the economy as a whole. The difference between savings and investments, therefore, is progressively reduced through wage increases, and the same thing happens with economic demand and economic supply, although only insofar as higher wages do not lead to price increases.

Only private demand is directly dependent upon income. The authorities finance their expenditure through taxes and levies and by borrowing. Thus the armament requirements and high consumption of the nobility, and later of nation states, as well as spending on public investments in infrastructure, education etc., have always represented a significant proportion of economic demand.[9] On many occasions, public demand has even enabled total economic demand to exceed economic supply.

The widening demand gap is mitigated by consumers borrowing money, and by more goods being exported than are imported. In addition, more and more capital is burned as speculation on the money market increases.

---

[9] See: Petersen: *Von der Staatswirtschaft zur Marktwirtschaft [From the State Economy to the Market Economy]* in: Wirtschaftsethik und Wirtschaftspolitik. Zur Überwindung der globalen Wirtschaftskrise. Von der liberalen zur sozialliberalen Wirtschaftsordnung [Economic Ethics and Economic Policy. On Overcoming the Global Economic Crisis. From the Liberal to the Social-Liberal Economic Order], p. 138ff.

Let's examine the components of the current capitalist secular stagnation!

3.1 Ever-increasing discrepancy between economic savings and profitable economic investment opportunities.

Only those who refrain from consuming are able to invest in the means of production. This means that rates of investment in less developed national economies are necessarily low. Economic growth leads to wage increases, making it possible to save more and more money which can then be used to finance capital goods.

However, saving alone is not enough to develop a national economy. Means of production must also be invented so that people can buy them. The more innovative production facilities and new products that are invented, the more savings can be spent on real economic investments.

When an economy has reached a certain degree of saturation yet continues to save increasing amounts, the risk will eventually arise that profitable innovations will lag behind savings and signs of stagnation will begin to emerge.

Bigger increases in saving tend to be seen when there is rising income inequality. Rising income inequality inevitably results from a situation in which the wealthy draw off additional income from their assets and reinvest it, and are able to save a disproportionately large amount due to their high incomes. The wealth of the super-rich grows without them even having to do anything. Their heirs start from a position of having a large amount of wealth and correspondingly high income from that wealth, and can continue to increase it disproportionately.

In 2007, according to various calculations by the German Institute for Economic Research, the richest 10% of the population over the age of 17 owned between 61 and 66% of all wealth, and the richest 0.1% (around 70,000 people) owned 1,627 billion Euros: almost a quarter of all wealth. The poorest half of the population, however (some 35 million people), owned 103 billion Euros - only 1.4% of all wealth - which is less than the ten richest people in Germany in the same year (with 113.7 billion).[10] Now, seven years on, the gap between rich and poor has widened further still. During the economic collapse of 2008/2009, assets naturally shrank considerably, but quickly recovered afterwards.

Wealth distribution
Adult population by tenths, proportions of total wealth in percent 2002 and 2007

Group	2002	2007
Richest tenth	57.9	61.1%
Second richest tenth	19.9	19.0 %
Third richest tenth	11.8	11.1 %
Fourth richest tenth	7.0	6.0 %
Fifth richest tenth	2.8	2.8 %
Sixth tenth	1.3	1.2 %
Seventh tenth	0.4	0.4 %
Eighth tenth	0.0	0.0 %
Ninth tenth	0.0	0.0 %
Tenth tenth	-1.2	-1.6 %

[11]

---

[10] http://de.wikipedia.org/wiki/Verm%C3%B6gensverteilung_in_Deutschland

[11] Joachim R. Frick and Markus M. Grabka: *Gestiegene Vermögensungleichheit in Deutschland [Increased Income Equality in Germany]* (PDF; 276 kB). In: Wochenbericht des DIW Berlin [Weekly Report by the German Institute for Economic Research Berlin], No. 4/2009, p. 59

Similarly, in the USA and Europe some 20% of income recipients earn 60% of economic income.

A basic condition for a healthy national economy is the balance of demand and supply on the market. When too few goods are supplied in relation to demand the result, as is well known, is inflation; when too many goods are supplied, the result is deflation, which then gives way to depression. What does this fundamental condition mean for the current relationship of supply and demand within national economies and in the global economy?

In the course of an economic period, incomes arise in proportion to goods and services, and these incomes must then purchase the goods and services that are being produced. If, owing to the current distribution of income, around 20% of all income recipients are earning roughly 60% of all income, then in order to preserve the balance of supply and demand on the market this 20% of earners must also spend 60% of income: i.e. they must consume or invest.

These 20% of income recipients will normally only spend a fraction of their income on consumption. The rest must be invested. The total funds to be invested also include the savings (albeit lower, per capita) of the remaining 80% of income recipients, which are naturally higher the more developed the national economy is.

Businesses invest directly in real goods (machinery etc.). The remaining savings are spent on securities, shares and bonds, or given out as loans: this includes savings funds made available to a bank. To preserve the balance of the market, the purchasing power transferred to others needs to reappear on the market in the form of demand for goods and services.

Understandably, entrepreneurs are only willing to make real economic investments if they can see lucrative investment opportunities. Furthermore, the investment behaviour of capitalists is different from that of small and medium-sized businesses and micro-entrepreneurs with assets, who actually have to use their investments to create capital income opportunities for themselves. This is why business start-ups, who do not have any collateral, often cannot get loans or, except for from so called 'business angels', financial shareholdings either. The results is that many useful investment opportunities are missed. This has already led to the creation of state institutions operating guarantee schemes, with the aim of helping small businesses to obtain capital.

The wealthy also treat their financial means less as real economic entrepreneurial opportunities than as play money, invested on a huge scale. Independently of the necessary innovations, major investments are also burdened with disproportionately large marketing and sales costs which can often be many times greater than the real economic investment and which of course are lost completely in the event of failure. This is why investors only invest in projects promising a return of at least 30%. Investing in a range of such 'start-ups' makes it possible to cope with failures. Naturally, when such extreme profit opportunities are not available there is a shortage of real economic investment and the real economy inevitably stagnates.

All investments ultimately aim at future consumption. This also applies to investment in machinery and capital goods, because capital goods are only purchased as long as they can ultimately be used to open up additional consumption opportunities in the national economy.

The sales potential of goods and services is fatally diminished, however, if income distribution shifts in favour of fewer people. This is because this shift causes an increase in economic savings and a corresponding reduction in purchasing power for the purposes for consumption. As a consequence, more and more must be invested for less and less consumer demand.

Savings rate in major industrial nations *)

Period	Germany 1)	Great Britain	France	USA	Japan
1950	4.2	-2.1	.	7.2	.
1951	4.0	-2.0	.	8.4	.
1952	6.6	-0.1	.	8.4	.
1953	7.6	0.3	.	8.3	.
1954	8.1	-0.5	.	7.6	.
1955	7.4	0.0	.	6.9	11.9
1956	6.6	1.9	.	8.5	12.9
1957	8.8	1.5	.	8.5	12.6

1958	9.1	0.7	.	8.6	12.3
1959	9.4	1.5	.	7.6	13.7
1960	9.2	4.1	16.8	7.3	17.4
1961	9.9	6.0	16.0	8.4	18.9
1962	9.5	5.0	18.5	8.3	18.7
1963	10.7	5.4	17.6	7.8	18.0
1964	11.8	6.5	17.4	8.8	18.7
1965	12.9	6.8	18.2	8.6	19.0
1966	12.3	7.1	17.7	8.3	18.4
1967	11.8	6.4	17.9	9.5	17.6
1968	13.1	5.5	17.6	8.4	20.3
1969	13.8	5.7	16.0	7.8	20.6
1970	14.7	6.5	21.2	9.4	19.7
1971	14.4	5.0	20.8	10.1	19.6
1972	15.3	7.3	21.4	8.9	20.0
1973	14.7	8.1	21.6	10.5	22.2
1974	15.6	8.4	22.4	10.6	24.4
1975	16.2	9.2	22.6	10.6	23.4
1976	14.5	8.7	20.7	9.4	23.5
1977	13.2	7.6	21.0	8.7	21.8
1978	13.3	9.4	22.4	8.9	20.9
1979	13.9	10.9	20.8	8.9	17.7
1980	13.1	12.3	19.7	10.0	17.3
1981	13.5	12.0	19.0	10.9	18.2
1982	12.9	10.8	18.3	11.2	16.8
1983	11.3	9.0	17.5	9.0	16.2
1984	11.8	10.2	15.9	10.8	16.1
1985	11.7	9.7	15.0	9.0	15.5
1986	12.5	8.1	14.3	8.2	14.8
1987	12.7	5.4	12.5	7.0	13.0
1988	13.1	3.9	12.9	7.3	13.5
1989	12.5	5.7	13.4	7.1	13.6
1990	13.7	8.1	14.0	7.0	13.9
1991	12.9	10.3	15.0	7.3	15.0
1992	12.7	11.7	15.7	7.7	14.2
1993	12.1	10.8	15.5	5.8	13.7
1994	11.4	9.3	14.7	4.8	12.6

1995	11.0	10.3	15.9	4.6	11.9
1996	10.5	9.4	15.0	4.0	10.6
1997	10.1	9.6	15.9	3.6	10.3
1998	10.1	7.4	15.5	4.3	11.3
1999	9.5	5.2	15.2	2.4	10.0
2000	9.2	4.7	15.1	2.9	8.7
2001	9.4	6.0	15.8	2.7	5.1
2002	9.9	4.8	16.9	3.5	5.0
2003	10.3	5.1	15.8	3.5	3.9
2004	10.4	3.7	15.8	3.4	3.6
2005	10.5	3.9	14.9	1.4	3.9
2006	10.5	2.9	15.1	2.4	3.8
2007	10.8	2.2	15.5	1.7	3.3
2008	11.2	1.7	15.3	2.7	.

Source: National Statistical Offices. Data available on: August 2009. –
* Savings as percent of private households' disposable income; level only partially comparable due to differing calculation methods. - 1 1950 - 1969 West Germany according to ESA '79; 1970 - 1990 West Germany according to ESA '95; from 1991 all of Germany according to ESA '95.[12]

Rising savings rates and corresponding rises in volumes of savings also require rising investment, because if the savings are not invested there will be a lack of economic demand and a national economy will stagnate until the economic savings are turned into investments. For a national economy in which not all workers are employed this means structural unemployment, which rises even further with every rationalisation investment.

Since the disparity between rising volumes of savings and private real economic investment opportunities has not evened out, and we have managed to avert depressions only through increases in state spending and export surpluses, we have been living, since the 1960s, in a state of secular stagnation.

---

[12] http://www.nachdenkseiten.de/upload/pdf/091030_hinweise_sparquote.pdf

3.2 How are surplus economic savings possible in relation to stagnating investment opportunities?

In relation to the goods and services being produced and supplied, surplus savings first became possible in the monetary economy - more precisely, with the emergence of the paper money economy. In a pure barter economy, income consists exclusively of manufactured products. Proportions of this income can also be saved up for harder times. But this saving, according to the criteria of modern economic theories, is also an investment, albeit in the form of an inventory investment. This also applies to the saving of gold, for example, or gold coins, since gold also has a material value.

Only in a paper money economy is it possible for somebody not to spend his or her share in manufactured products (which takes the form of salaries, rents, profits etc., paid out in paper money) but to save it in the form of paper money.

Classical capitalist economic theory maintained that it was safe to disregard this possibility, which could only arise if somebody did not take his or her savings to the bank but instead kept them 'under the mattress' - (i.e. at home). Any sensible person, however, is expected to invest his or her money or take it to the bank, which then lends it out and passes on part of its profits to savers in the form of interest.

A so-called *liquidity preference*, or the parking of paper money, was first introduced into economic theory by *John Maynard Keynes* as a rational motive in the event of falling prices in economic downturns, when it is expected that more will be able to be purchased with the money later on. The same applies to investments. If not much is being invested due to an economic downturn, interest rates remain low. It can therefore be profitable to keep one's capital liquid and only to invest when the economy picks up again and interest rates rise. It can also be useful, given the potential losses that may be sustained as a result of the economic downturn, to keep hold of a liquidity reserve.

But even in economic theory, 'investing in money', which is not in the proper sense a real economic investment, is only a temporary phenomenon, which will dissolve again during the next boom phase, if not before. Our current global economic problems, however, are not an economic phenomenon; they are of a structural nature. This means we are suffering not from *temporary* but from *structural* stagnation. According to Paul Krugman, there have been no economic boom phases (in the proper sense of the term) in the global economy since the 1990s, unless you count the dotcom and property speculation bubbles as economic booms.

In Paul Krugman's words: 'We now know that the economic expansion of 2003-2007 was driven by a bubble. You can say the same about the latter part of the 90s expansion; and you can in fact say the same about the later years of the Reagan expansion, which was driven at that point by runaway thrift institutions and a large bubble in commercial real estate.'[13] The cause of the tendency for more to be saved than can usefully be invested in real economic projects is simply not considered by neoclassical economics.

3.3 The tendency for rationalisation investments to outweigh consumer goods innovations and expansion

Rationalisation investments tend to outweigh expansion investments and the production of new consumer goods. This was how the Industrial Revolution began, in fact. Traditional methods of production such as those used by weavers were replaced initially by mechanised and eventually by steam-powered production methods, which led to unemployment and poverty in traditional craft enterprises.

It is easier to increase profit through rationalisation investments than by developing new consumer goods, and investing in expansion only makes sense if the number of potential buyers is rising. Developing new products requires high levels of expenditure on development. The introduction of new products also calls for special marketing efforts. With rationalisation investments, on the other hand, the savings made by axing salaries are turned directly into capital assets, minus ongoing depreciation on investments of course.

---

[13] Paul Krugman: *Secular Stagnation, Coalmines, Bubbles, and Larry Summers,* in New York Times November 16, 2013.

When more workers are laid off as a result of rationalisation investments than are taken on as a result of investment in innovation and expansion, consumer demand drops because workers are earning less, and earners on higher incomes do not increase their consumption in line with those incomes but tend to save instead.

Pure rationalisation investments lead to workers being replaced by machines and more productive means of production. What was previously earned by workers is then earned by employers and investors. If these employers and investors do not then spend their additional income and thus compensate for the lack of demand from the workers who have been laid off, signs of depression start to emerge. The fewer opportunities there are to invest in new products or expansion, the greater the risk of depression.

In the event of insufficient innovation and investment in expansion, production costs fall not only as a result of rationalisation investments but also as a result of the drop in wage costs when widespread rationalisation investments lead to increased unemployment and thus to falling wages. Employers' and capitalists' income share in gross national product increases accordingly, and this tends to widen the gap between economic demand and economic supply.

As outlined above, the economy's own development tendencies led it, even after the Industrial Revolution and the advent of capitalism, into a state of secular stagnation. This tendency, however, was masked by demand developments which are not, or which are only partly, compatible with the capitalist economic model.

3.4 Ways of compensating for the demand gap in a national economy through wage increases, state spending, increasing consumer debt, capital exports and burning capital.

3.4.1 Ways of compensating for the demand gap in a national economy through wage increases

During the initial industrialisation of a nation, the introduction of new methods of production will usually have caused workers to be laid off, leading to unemployment, unless surplus goods were able to be exported. It is not without significance, therefore, that the beginning of the Industrial Revolution in European countries was marked by a mercantile foreign trade policy which promoted export.

Japan too was able to compensate for a domestic drop in demand for goods and services using export surpluses. The same applies to China, which has built up a global market for its consumer goods production and is able to employ domestic workers because the manufactured goods can be exported on a very large scale.

Where advances in productivity are accompanied by sufficient wage increases, which are spent mainly on consumption, the danger of demand shortages is naturally lessened. With the advent of industrialisation, when the tendency was for more workers to be laid off than were being taken on, the excess supply of labour meant that general wage increases were only possible once the workers had organised themselves into trade unions and pushed for higher wages through industrial action.

The rising skill levels of workers in developing countries, however, has led more and more businesses to relocate wage-intensive production to these countries. Developing countries also represent new, unsaturated markets. This has resulted in rising unemployment in industrialised nations, with the result that domestic trade unions are losing the power to push for higher wages, and the wage level is falling to the level found in developing countries.

Naturally, it is unskilled workers who are affected first and most seriously by this development. For more highly qualified workers, whose skills are still not yet sufficiently widespread in developing countries, pay is still rising. Thus we see a growing disparity not only between the incomes of workers on the one hand and employers and capitalists on the other, but also between the incomes of skilled and unskilled workers.

We are also seeing more and more production facilities requiring more highly skilled staff relocating to other countries, and this is not just because the skill level of the workforce in developing countries (particularly in emerging countries) is rising. At time goes on, countries with large markets like China, India, Brazil and Russia will put increasing pressure on businesses in the industrialised nations to set up skilled production plants in these countries even when production costs there are higher than in old industrialised countries, but when the market is threatened by exports from the industrialised countries.

In the industrialised nations, this will mean that excess domestic savings will be less and less restricted by rising wages, making it possible to prevent secular stagnation turning into crises.

3.4.2. Ways of compensating for the demand gap in a national economy through state spending

In technological terms, a huge number of productive forces and new products were made possible by the Industrial Revolution. The products could only be economically produced and sold, however, when there was sufficient purchasing power. At the beginning of the Industrial Revolution, as in the period leading up to it, it was the nobility and newly rich members of the bourgeoisie who exercised this purchasing power. The purchasing power of the working population, on the other hand, initially decreased due to the preponderance of rationalisation investments, and did not start to pick up until later on. So it was always the wealthy, and the state in particular, whose demand for goods and services first enabled the economic implementation of technological inventions, and from then on they continued to be a crucial factor in ensuring sufficient economic demand. Expenditure on military and armaments requirements, then on infrastructure, and eventually on welfare, made up a large proportion of economic demand and even drove economic demand higher than supply in times of political tension or war.

In order to prevent workers on the lowest wages from being left behind or even impoverished, a system of social transfer had to be developed. This made it possible to prevent too great an erosion of consumer demand.

The increasing importance of state spending for economic demand is shown in the following table:

>>Development of public spending 1900 - 1975

	Germany*	USA**	Great Britain
1900	12.3		14.4
1913	15.4	8.5	12.4
1922		12.6	27.8
1927	24.8	11.7	24.1
1930	26.9	12.3	26.2
1934	34.7	19.8	24.5
1937	35.0	16.6	25.7
1950	31.3	21.3	39.0
1974	35.6	32.5	46.7
1975	38.6	35.0	

* *Expenditure by all local authorities (up to 1949; direct expenditure; from 1950: total expenditure) as a proportion of net national product at market prices.*
** *Expenditure by all local authorities as a proportion of gross national product at market prices.*<<[14]

According to the Federal Ministry of Finance, public spending including social security (17.7%) already stood at 48.8% of gross national product by 1975.[15]

Looking at the amount of state spending and social transfer as a proportion of total economic demand and the intrinsic tendency toward stagnation in capitalist economic development, as outlined above, it becomes very clear that had this public expenditure not existed as a source of demand, economic development would not have been possible. State spending is funded by taxes, principally collected from those on higher incomes, and by public debt. Both

---

[14] See: Willi Albers, Anton Zottmann: *Hdb. der Wirtschaftswissenschaften [Economics Handbook]*, p. 363.
[15] Spending by the state in national accounts. From 1970 in the European System of Accounts (ESA 1995), Federal Ministry of Finance - I A 4 25 February 2014
http://www.bundesfinanzministerium.de/Content/DE/Standardartikel/Themen/Oeffentliche_Finanzen/Wirtschafts_und_Finanzdaten/Oeffentlicher_Gesamthaushalt/entwicklung-der-staatsquote-anl.pdf?

these sources of funds represent a siphoning-off of excess purchasing power and thus a reduction in savings in the economy, and the redirection of those savings into economic demand. If these funds had not been siphoned off, a much larger amount would have had to be invested, which would not have been possible due to the way profitable innovations lag behind savings.[16]

Where state spending is financed by borrowing, public debt rises. This was why - to cite just a few examples - public debt[17] in 2013 amounted to 108% of gross national product in the USA, 81% in Germany, 88% in the UK, 91% in France and as much as 245% in Japan.

This debt development has problematic implications. Financing public spending using public debt leads to the circulation of government bonds, and the greater the circulation, the less can ever be paid back. In practice, loans due for repayment are usually just extended - old debts are refinanced by new debts, in other words. This means that governments' ability to repay public debt is dependent upon investors' willingness to refinance. If they are not willing to do this, as experience has shown, the consequence is state bankruptcies. The level of public debt is substantially reduced only in exceptional cases - when oil licensing revenues arise, for example, as happened in England and Norway with the exploitation of North Sea oil.

But even if a state wanted to cut expenditure in order to repay its debts, to do so in periods of secular stagnation would be to stall economic growth even further, since reduced state spending would lead to a drop in economic demand. The creditors whose purchasing power would be increased by the repaid state loans would lack alternative investment opportunities, thus widening the gap between higher economic savings and economic supply.

---

[16] For a more detailed discussion of the importance of public authorities in the development of demand, see: *Uwe Petersen: Wirtschaftsethik und Wirtschaftspolitik...[Economic Ethics and Economic Policy...]*, p. 180ff.
[17] Source: © Statista 2014

As the quantity of public bonds in circulation increases, there is too little consideration of the fact that they do not, in practice, represent any material value. The savings on which they are based are turned into public expenditure and thus back into economic consumption, and are thereby *burned* as savings funds.

State investments are also, in practice, a form of public consumption. Otherwise they would have to be amortised over the course of their use and the amortisation amounts would have to be retained for repayment or renewal. They are treated, however, like the purchase of a passenger car, as immediately depreciable expenditure. In other words, the creditors of national debt consider themselves, as owners of securities, to be wealthy, when in fact they are the holders of *toxic assets*.

If public loans are taken out in order to bail out banks, and these funds are later repaid by the banks, public debt may be reduced to some extent. The total quantity of circulating bonds, however, remains dangerously high: the danger lies in the fact that the bonds can be used to speculate against nations and currencies.

3.4.3 Ways of compensating for the demand gap in a national economy through capital export

It is usually desirable for a national economy that the country's savings should be reinvested, creating more jobs, or that the economy should become more efficient as a result of rationalisation investments. If, however, the distribution of income in a country has shifted so far in favour of the few highest earners that the goods produced can no longer all be sold within that country, and consumer demand in the country is also too low to purchase goods and services from abroad, then export surpluses may result. Export surpluses are always tantamount to granting credit to foreign nations in the amount of the export surplus - in other words, capital/savings are exported in the amount of the export surplus.[18]

---

[18] Strictly speaking, a distinction must be drawn between the export of capital to fund foreign investments (when property, shares, companies or facilities abroad are purchased for a country's own companies), and the granting of credit to foreign companies and governments. In the narrower

So countries like Germany and China, for example, are able to use their export surpluses to neutralise surplus purchasing power through foreign purchases. But this was not without also burning a large amount of capital. In this way, according to a study by the German Institute for Economic Research, 'German investors have lost around 400 billion Euros through bad investments abroad, equivalent to roughly 15 percent of gross domestic product. From 2006 to 2012 the figure was even higher, at around 600 billion Euros - that is 22 percent of gross domestic product.'[19] German investors also 'made 200 billion Euros profit from 1999 to 2006.'[20] The losses over the period from 1999 to 2012 take into account this initial profit.

In a national economy, the economic relationship between supply and demand is balanced out by export surpluses and this stops the country slipping into economic depression. On the global economic level, however, other countries must take on debt if people or businesses from the export surplus country do not invest in the

---

sense, foreign countries are only in debt if they have borrowed money. However, if the economy of a country in which other nations have invested starts to deteriorate, the foreign capital can be withdrawn from the country very quickly - as was seen in the Asian financial crisis of 1997/98, for example. Wirtschaftslexikon24.net has this to say of the crisis: 'The Asian crisis of 1997/98 is an example of how country-specific causes and factors relating to foreign trade and investment can lead to the decline of an entire region. Currency speculation, lax banking supervision and crony capitalism triggered the crisis and led to a sharp downturn in the national economies that were affected (particularly in Thailand, where the crisis began in the summer of 1997, but also in Indonesia, South Korea, Malaysia, Taiwan, the Philippines and Hong Kong). Inflation, currency depreciation and economic decline were the result. Currency devaluations (such as in Indonesia, of up to 80 percent) led to imported inflation, while foreign investors hastily withdrew financial resources. Social unrest resulted.'
(http://www.wirtschaftslexikon24.net/d/asienkrise/asienkrise.htm)

[19] Stefan Bach et al: *Deutschland muss mehr in seine Zukunft investieren [Germany Must Invest More in its Future]*, in: DIW Wochenbericht [Weekly Report by the German Institute for Economic Research Berlin], No. 26.2013, p.3.

[20] Further information about the German Institute for Economic Research is available upon request by email.

import surplus country themselves. For import surplus countries, this incurs an obligation to pay back the imported capital with interest, including supplier loans.

If the net capital export in subsequent economic periods is reduced as a result of these payments, however, the economic demand gap in the export surplus country will widen again. The only way to prevent a reduction in the net capital export from causing a depression is for the country to reduce its export surpluses accordingly, i.e. to export less or import more.

Both these things, however, are contingent upon an increase in demand in the export surplus country. Given that consumption in a stagnating economy can rarely increase sufficiently, due partly to the relatively high level of income but even more to the unequal distribution of income, and given that, as a result, domestic investments can rarely be expanded, the only other option is an increase in state consumption, funded by higher taxes or higher debt. In the latter case, state spending would replace capital export in order to compensate for the gap in domestic demand. We will look later on at how difficult it is to get rid of a chronic export surplus, by studying the example of Germany.

Given that export surpluses can be used to compensate for the domestic demand gap in an open economy, *Gablers Wirtschaftslexikon [Gabler's Economic Lexicon]* states: The argument for the emergence of secular stagnation 'seems plausible in the case of closed economies. In open economies, the accumulation of excess savings would flow abroad, cause devaluation of the domestic currency and, via an increase in goods exports, trigger an expansionary multiplier process. A decline in domestic national income need not then occur.'[21]

The objection that secular stagnation cannot occur in an open economy fails to convince, however, when all industrialised nations are suffering from secular stagnation and developing countries, despite high growth rates, are failing to absorb enough excess savings, partly because they cannot borrow excessive amounts. In

---

[21] Hans-Werner Wohltmann: *Säkulare Stagnation [Secular Stagnation]* in:http://wirtschaftslexikon.gabler.de/Definition/saekulare-stagnation.html

developing countries, moreover, there are extreme disparities in wealth and income, stemming from feudal structures, and these disparities can be massively exacerbated by pioneering entrepreneurs (as we have seen in recent economic history with the oligarchs of Eastern Europe). This means that not even the savings within these countries themselves can be fully invested there, with the result that they too suffer from a tendency towards stagnation.

The very first industrialised nations found that they had to export more goods than they imported, because there was not enough domestic demand backed by purchasing power to support the new industries. The same goes for the development of Japan, and most recently China, which both have high export surpluses and need to export corresponding amounts of capital in order to balance out supply and demand at home.

Another potential consequence of secular stagnation is that manufacturing operations may be moved abroad without enough new jobs being created to employ all the workers who have been laid off. The wealthy upper classes do not seek to challenge this. They can earn their money abroad, and import goods which are not or no longer available at home. Job cuts in conjunction with import surpluses is the worst form of secular stagnation.

3.4.4 Ways of compensating for the demand gap in a national economy by burning capital

When real economic investments are exceeded by savings which are not invested in government securities or distributed in the form of consumer loans or transferred abroad as capital exports, the only other option is the speculative capital market. Revenues on the speculative capital market largely consist of shifts in stock values (shares, property, gold, commodities, currencies, artworks etc.); speculators exploit exchange rate differences where possible, or bet on expected price developments. With the increase in their wealth and tradeable old stocks and securities, and ultimately derivatives, the wealthy tend to lose their emotional connection to material assets, and capitalist behaviour, with its profit-maximising gambles on the capital market, tends to degenerate.[22]

For investors as a whole, it is a zero-sum game. What some of them win, the others lose, unless prices are driven up by expectations and the pressure to invest. This results in capital gains for everyone, but these gains are lost when prices fall again.

Profits on the speculative capital market are diminished by the commissions and charges paid to banks and financial services providers, and their incomes are considerable - so considerable, in fact, that in the peak periods of speculation they accounted for 40% of all entrepreneurial profits in the USA. The financial services providers had amassed such a level of wealth that they spent their profits generously and savings rates fell to almost 0%.[23] In amounts equal to the remuneration paid to financial services providers, savings were also turned back into consumer spending: in other words, burnt as capital. Many people naturally used increases in the value of shares, property and other material assets to increase their consumption. Thus real estate owners during the American property speculation phase took out consumer loans

---

[22] For more details see: Uwe Petersen: *Wie die Unternehmenskultur zur Shareholder Value Mentalität degenerierte und Kapitalisten zu Heuschrecken wurden [How Corporate Culture Degenerated into Shareholder Value Mentality and Capitalists Became Locusts]*, in: Unkonventionelle Betrachtungsweisen zur Wirtschaftskrise: Von Haien, Heuschrecken und anderem Getier. [Unconventional Views on the Economic Crisis: On Sharks, Locusts and Other Animals] p.69ff. and *Die Verwandlung der Leistungsträger von großen Tieren zu Schmeißfliegen des Kapitalmarktes wurden [The Transformation of Service Providers from the Big Fish to the Blowflies of the Capital Market]*, in: loc. cit. p.75ff. and *Die schleichende Zerstörung der Wirtschaftsethik [The Insidious Destruction of Economic Ethics]* in: loc. cit. p. 81ff.

[23] For more details see: Petersen: *Die zunehmende Finanzialisierung und Shareholder-Value-Orientierung [Increasing Financialisation and Shareholder Value Orientation]* in: Wirtschaftsethik und Wirtschaftspolitik. Zur Überwindung der globalen Wirtschaftskrise. Von der liberalen zur sozialliberalen Wirtschaftsordnung [Economic Ethics and Economic Policy. On Overcoming the Global Economic Crisis. From the Liberal to the Social-Liberal Economic Order], p. 212 ff.

equivalent to the increases in the value of their real estate. Also the realisation of speculative increases in the value of shares probably generated additional consumption. In this way, then, savings can be turned back into consumer spending.

Capital burning through the consumption of financial services providers and through increases in value is not sufficient, however, to balance demand and supply in industrialised nations and to achieve a relatively high level of employment. In order to make full use of the economy's capacity, the demand for speculative real economic purchases must be stimulated. Real estate is particularly suitable for this. The so-called 'dotcom' speculative boom, which saw huge investment in potentially innovative young companies, also stimulated the economy. With the bursting of the speculative bubble, the excess savings were then offset by corresponding losses. When inflated asset prices fall again, the final holders of the assets end up footing the bill for the funds that have flowed back into consumption.

Where capital investments are financed with an investor's own resources, the devaluation of intangible assets need not affect the economy very much. But problems arise when capital investments are financed with borrowed funds which, once assets become devalued, can no longer be repaid. This can lead, as in the last real estate crisis, to significant economic disruptions, with banks classed as '*too big to fail*' having to be bailed out to prevent the economic movement of payments from coming to a standstill.

Due to the necessity of turning capital back into real economic purchases, in periods without speculative bubbles we generally tend to experience depressed economic activity, unless excess savings can, as in Germany, be neutralised by capital exports or unless governments take the excess savings out of the market via bonds for additional state spending. Speculative bubbles are certainly not a sign that secular stagnation has been overcome. They only stop it giving way to a depression, or postpone this process. Meanwhile sky-rocketing prices on the stock exchanges, so often celebrated in the news, climb higher and higher and hit target after target, but at the same time the fragility of the economy, and with it the risk of another crisis, steadily increases.

As we have already seen, the capital market is also flooded with government bonds without any material value. Speculative bubbles against or for a country can cause considerable economic problems internationally. Devaluations of government bonds cause interest rates to rise, in which case a country may borrow more or may be refused further credit; this can lead to national bankruptcy.

If capital then flees to more highly valued currencies, as happened in spectacular fashion with the Swiss franc, for example, the countries in question have to implement foreign exchange controls, or extend the money supply enough to avoid any adverse effects on their ability to export. In any case, currencies themselves are also speculative values to a large extent. Saving in money leads directly to a corresponding fall in demand for real economic goods and services.

Because all investments traded on the capital market, including shares and real estate and their derivatives, as well as gold and commodities, have recently tended to become short-term objects of speculation, a longer term investment structure in the capital market is no longer possible, and is becoming less possible by the day. Any investment can be exchanged for any other, with incalculable dangers for the economy as a whole. None of us can consider ourselves safe, therefore, not even in Germany.

II. Stages of secular stagnation since the 1960s and the economic measures taken to combat its symptoms whilst simultaneously increasing the fragility of the economic system

1. The beginnings of modern secular stagnation following the end of the postwar reconstruction period

The last big surge in demand in Europe was in the postwar period, when the damage caused by the war was repaired and it became possible to meet the demand which it had been impossible to meet during the war years. The economic structure that would be necessary in order to do this was already familiar, and needed only to be resurrected - and consumers were already familiar with the food products and consumer goods they had lacked during the war, meaning that no special marketing efforts were needed in order to introduce new products to the market. In addition, new products and production techniques had been developed during the war years, in the USA in particular, inspired in large part by military research. These new products could now be sold too.

At that time there was no danger that too much of national income would be saved and thus withdrawn as demand from the market. On the contrary: wages had to remain low so that profits would be as high as possible, and could then be used for investment. This proved possible due to the fact that industry was not able to immediately re-employ all the available workers, meaning that there was no opportunity to push for higher wages. The trade unions recognised, too, that the most important thing initially was to re-establish production capacity - only then would it be possible for higher wages to be paid.

Demand was so strong that even high taxes did not curb it. Meanwhile, the state was not spending all of its income. In Germany, for example, in stark contrast to today's steadily mounting government debt, huge revenue surpluses were achieved, and an equivalent amount of demand was withdrawn from the market. 'Under the Adenauer government, Fritz Schäffer managed to put aside eight billion marks (equivalent to around 35 billion Euros today) 'for a rainy day'.'[24] The federal budget surpluses accumulated in Germany from 1953 to 1957 were dubbed the *Juliusturm*[25].

The USA provided European countries with revolving capital funds in the form of US dollars as part of the Marshall Plan, which enabled these European countries - whose gold reserves had evaporated in the world war and whose currencies were worth nothing internationally, and could not be converted - to import the latest technology from abroad, particularly from the USA. In doing this, of course, the USA was also supporting its own economy, which since the end of the war had experienced a drop in the demand for armaments and war supplies.

---

[24] http://de.wikipedia.org/wiki/Juliusturm.
[25] http://de.wikipedia.org/wiki/Juliusturm, 'The name refers to a 32-metre fortified tower of the Spandau Citadel [Berlin]'. Part of the 'imperial war chest[from the war with France from 1870 to 1871], 120 million marks in gold coins was stored in the Juliusturm until 1914.'

With the beginning of the Cold War, the Korean War and later the Vietnam War, public demand in the USA, but also in Britain and France, picked up again so strongly that the USA's export surpluses became import surpluses. This acted as a stimulus for German exports. Germany and Japan in particular built up increasing export surpluses, which is synonymous with additional demand financed by capital export (i.e. the export of savings).

And once full employment was reached, higher wages were introduced. This too led to an increase in domestic demand. In the 1960s, however, as basic consumer demand was increasingly satisfied, savings rates went up, and as they did so the gap between economic savings and investments widened.

When, in spite of high export surpluses and corresponding capital exports, the point was reached where not all savings could be fully invested, economic policy recalled the anti-cyclical fiscal policy of John Maynard Keynes and increased state spending to compensate for the lack of economic demand.

In order to do this, the accumulated revenue surpluses were dismantled; the Juliusturm was plundered. Then public borrowing steadily increased. According to the anti-cyclical theory, the additional debts incurred in order to increase state spending are supposed be offset by revenue surpluses generated by lower state spending in the expected phase of economic recovery. This, however, did not happen, and not only because politicians like to spend higher revenues on their voters in the form of tax cuts or subsidies or spectacular structures designed to act as monuments to their greatness. Because of the shortfall in general investment on the back of the savings, the additional demand is still needed - in other words, we no longer experience pronounced boom and bust phases in the classical sense. There is a good reason, therefore - given that public spending is not financed exclusively by government revenue - why public debt has been steadily mounting right up to the present day.

The Federal Republic of Germany's total debt in 1950 stood at €9.6 billion. It had risen to €29 billion by 1960, to €64.2 billion by 1970, to €238.9 billion by 1980, to €538.3 billion by 1990, to

€1,210.9 billion by 2000 and to €2,011.7 billion in 2010.[26] Despite all the talk of enforcing a debt brake, by 2012 the debt had risen by a further €56.6 billion to €2,068.3 billion.

2. Stagflation

Because the classical economic theorists and economic policymakers did not realise that the economy had been in a state of secular stagnation since the 1960s, they were surprised by the fact that since the end of that decade, despite inflationary price development, the economy had been stagnating and could not be adequately controlled even using monetary policy measures and an anti-cyclical spending policy. In fact, tight monetary policy actually heightened unwanted depressive tendencies.

Since the end of the 1960s, therefore, we have been faced with a previously unknown combination of stagnation and inflation. The term 'stagflation' has been invented to describe this phenomenon. It is defined on Wikipedia as follows: 'During a phase of stagflation, an economy is unable to maximise the use of productive capacity by supplying more money or granting credit facilities, nor is it able to reduce the excessive rate of currency devaluation through lower levels of activity. These two goals are mutually exclusive and thus pose an economic policy dilemma.

This phenomenon, unknown anywhere in the world until the end of the 1960s, was first observed in 1969 in Britain and and USA. The term was also used in Germany in the early 1970s (in the run-up to the 1972 parliamentary election), to describe comparatively long-lasting economic stagnation (not underemployment) and a comparatively high rate of inflation.'[27]

The phenomenon of secular stagnation as a growing discrepancy between economic savings and profitable investments was still not understood - it was thought that the cause of inflation was not a

---

[26] https://www.destatis.de/DE/ZahlenFakten/GesellschaftStaat/Oeffentliche Finanzen-Steuern/OeffentlicheFinanzen/Schulden/Tabellen/SchuldenNichtOeffentlich_Insgesamt.html

[27] http://de.wikipedia.org/wiki/Stagflation.

general increase in demand but an increase in costs. However, although stagflation was observed 'at the end of the 1960s in Britain and the USA', secular stagnation was blamed solely on the raising of oil prices by OPEC in 1973. As is well known, OPEC cut oil production, to quote Wikipedia, 'in 1973 as a result of political tensions in the Middle East, thus doubling the price of oil in just two years (1973-75) and creating a cost explosion in western industrialised nations. The inflation rate in the USA almost doubled in 1974 (from 6 % to 11 %). In the following year (1975) the unemployment rate in the USA rose to 8.4%, meaning that it too had almost doubled in relation to the rate in 1973 (when it stood at 4.9%).'[28]

Analyses of stagflation did not pay enough attention to the significance of rising wage costs at that time: businesses were passing these costs on to customers in the form of higher prices. Employment was relatively high, at least in the major industrialised countries. These countries still had strong trade unions, which not only kept wages rising in line with company profits, but also wanted to improve the distribution of income so as to help workers on the lowest incomes, and pushed through higher and higher wages and reductions in working hours. Businesses responded with corresponding price increases, which in turn led the trade unions to negotiate further wage increases. The consequence was wage-price spirals, or price-wage spirals, depending on your point of view.

Again, monetary policy was helpless in the face of inflation caused by cost increases. Whenever it capped the money supply and/or raised interest rates, it triggered signs of depression, and when central banks eased monetary policy again, cost inflation accelerated.

And the huge increases in the price of oil contributed not only to a general rise in prices but also to stagnation. Apart from the immediate shock affecting the entire price structure of all energy-dependent industrial goods, the oil price increases also caused a shift in purchasing power from consumers to oil-exporting countries. Demand was withdrawn from the market at a level equivalent to the oil price increases because the oil-exporting countries, naturally, were not immediately able to feed their increased revenues

---

[28] http://de.wikipedia.org/wiki/Stagflation.

back into the market in the form of spending. The size of the demand gap in the global economy was thus increased, at least in the short and medium term.

I discuss the phenomenon of stagflation in more depth in the book: *Arbeitslosigkeit unser Schicksal? Wirtschaftspolitik in der Stagflation [Are We Doomed to Unemployment? Economic Policy in Stagflation]*[29].

3. The end of the inflation within stagflation through deindustrialisation

Initially, industrialised countries used developing countries solely as suppliers of commodities and as sales markets. They held no appeal as production sites because they did not have enough skilled workers. Because these countries imported more than they exported, their level of debt mounted despite all the development aid they received. This forced them to regulate their imports more strictly, and they increasingly demanded that only countries that were prepared to produce within developing countries should be allowed to sell imports to them.

It was relatively easy to relocate contract manufacturing - in the textile industry, for example - to developing countries, because it required only minimal training of the workforce. For more highly skilled production, these demands were initially felt to be onerous, but the exporters had to comply with them where the market was large enough to warrant it. At first, however, they relocated only partial functions of their operations. The packaging and assembly of products, for example, was relocated to developing countries. The pharmaceutical companies set up 'finishing plants' in developing countries, where pills were manufactured from raw materials and packaged.

But over time, even this simple labour-intensive manufacturing work created a more skilled workforce. And this workforce, because its wages were so much lower, made relocating more highly skilled production to these countries an ever more attractive prospect.

---

[29] Verlag Peter Lang Frankfurt am Main Bern New York 1985.

Naturally, in the course of these relocations, the employment rate in the industrialised nations fell, particularly for less skilled workers. The growth or threat of unemployment made it more and more difficult for the unions to push for higher wages; in fact, incomes actually fell as time went on. And as cheaper raw materials began to be imported, mining in the industrialised nations was abandoned. This caused many job losses, particularly in mining regions such as the Ruhr area and Saarland.

The price increases resulting from wage-price spirals were particularly drastic in Britain where, unlike in Germany, there were no sector-wide trade unions - instead, every profession had its own trade union and negotiated its own wage increases. This meant that strikes by just a few skilled workers within a business could cripple entire sectors.

Margaret Thatcher, elected as prime minister in 1979, broke the power of the unions. Wikipedia states: 'The key event was the 1984-5 UK miners' strike against planned pit closures and privatisation. The strike lasted a year. The National Union of Mineworkers (NUM) had soon exhausted its reserves ('strike funds'), leaving it unable to offer any strike pay. Many miners got into debt as a result. Eventually, on 3 March, a NUM delegates' conference voted to end the industrial action.

Thatcher's "victory" caused lasting damage to the influence of English trade unions. This left the way clear for further reforms such as the abolition of the 'closed shop' (the legal obligation to become a member of a trade union, which had applied to workers in many companies) and the prohibition of so-called 'flying pickets' (mobile pickets that were not attached to the picketed location).([30]) During Thatcher's first term in office, the unemployment rate rose to three million at its peak in 1983 (around 12.5%).'[31]

---

[30] Franz-Josef Brüggemeier: *Geschichte Grossbritanniens im 20. Jahrhundert [A History of Britain in the 20th Century]*, p. 323, published by C.H. Beck, Munich 2010.

[31] http://de.wikipedia.org/wiki/Margaret_Thatcher.

In 1980, completely misjudging the causes of stagflation, incoming US president Ronald Reagan thought he could combat inflation using tight monetary policy whilst at the same time stimulating investors' willingness to invest, and with it economic activity, by cutting taxes.

Rainer Hank writes: 'Reagan - and his brilliant Fed chairman Paul Volcker - rid the world of the scourge of inflation. ... In 1980 prices in America had risen by eleven percent; by 1982, inflation had been cut to less than four percent. This came at the cost of blood, sweat and tears which, in monetary policy terms, took the form of a short but severe recession at the beginning of the 1980s. It was triggered by a sudden reduction in the money supply, marked by interest rate rises, and the curbing of the trade unions' power to negotiate pay. From then on, employees were no longer able to drive up the rate of inflation with high wage settlements.'[32]

Eugene Jarecki explains: 'With the *Economic Recovery Tax Act of 1981*, the Reagan administration slashed the top rate of income tax from 70% to 33%. Capital gains tax and corporate taxes were also cut. This led to a considerable loss of tax revenues.[33]'. In addition to this, 'spending on welfare programmes was also... cut ([34]).'[35]

The results of this policy were described in *Der Spiegel* on 4/10/1982: 'After just two years in office, the US president has set a second lamentable record: Following the steep rise in unemployment, which in July reached its highest peak for over 40 years, the number of companies going bankrupt is now soaring: In the period to September of this year, 473 companies went bankrupt every week - numbers the like of which we have not seen since the

---

[32] Rainer Hank: *Der amerikanische Virus [The American Virus]*, Karl Blessing Verlag 2009, p. 46f.

[33] Office of Tax Analysis: *Revenue Effects of Major Tax Bills*. (PDF) 2003, rev. September 2006. Working Paper 81, Table 2. Accessed on 5 February 2011

[34] *Ronald Reagan - Geliebt und gehasst [Ronald Reagan - Loved and Hated]*, a documentary by Eugene Jarecki (also available online)

[35] http://de.wikipedia.org/wiki/Reaganomics

Great Depression of the 1930s. In spite of all the tax breaks and business-friendly conditions, there was an increase in the number of bankruptcies of around 50% on the preceding year.'[36]

Because the economy was in a state of secular stagnation - i.e. savings were too high in relation to real economic investment opportunities - monetary policy restrictions naturally took full effect. As a result of the tax cuts, the excess savings were boosted even further without this leading to increased investment opportunities. If the tax cuts had resulted in reduced state expenditure, the economic slump would have been even more severe. Expenditure increased, however, as a result of government debt. 'By the end of 1988, government debt under Reagan had risen by 179.6% by the end of 1988 to 2.6 billion dollars.[37],[38]

There was little regret among the British and American policymakers of the time about loss of industrial jobs. On the contrary, this was even seen as a sign that the economy was developing because it was on its way to becoming a service economy - in other words, the lost industrial jobs would be not only replaced but overcompensated for by jobs in the service sector. Thus, as Rohleder writes, 'in recent years the tertiary sector in the USA, Japan and Germany has become the dominant driver of growth. In the period from 1970 to 1975, the service sector accounted for between 59 and 64% of economic growth. Since the beginning of the 1990s this percentage has risen to at least 85% in the countries surveyed; in Germany and Japan, in the period from 1990 - 1994, it accounted for almost all growth, standing at 91%.'[39]

---

[36] *Reaganomics - kein Vorbild [Reaganomics - a Bad Example]*, http://www.spiegel.de/spiegel/print/d-14348704.html

[37] Historical Debt Outstanding – Annual 1950–2000

[38] http://de.wikipedia.org/wiki/Ronald_Reagan

[39] Christoph Rohleder: *Globalisierung, Tertiarisierung und multinationale Unternehmen - Eine international vergleichende Analyse zur Diskordanz von wirtschaftlicher und politischer Entwicklung [Globalisation, Tertiarisation and Multinational Companies - an International Comparative Analysis of the Discordance of Economic and Political Development]* -, Cologne Dissertation 2004, p. 129.

It was initially thought that services were rationalisation-resistant. Bernd Bienzeisler writes: 'The debate about services begins with the *three sector theory*, which dates back to a book published by Colin Clark ([40]) and entitled *The Conditions of Economic Progress*. At the heart of the theory is the hypothesis that in the course of economic growth employment shifts from the primary sector (agriculture) to the secondary sector (industry) and finally to the tertiary sector (all other services). ... Differences in productivity developments are seen as justification for the theory. As the primary and particularly the secondary sector achieve higher and higher productivity as a result of mechanisation and automation, workers are laid off. These workers find permanent employment in the tertiary sector, firstly because demand in this sector is constantly on the rise thanks to economic growth, and secondly because output cannot be increased in the same way. Thanks to the 'uno acto principle', tertiary sector activity is to a certain extent 'rationalisation-resistant'[[41]].'([42])

'Building on the three sector theory, Jean Fourastié [[43]], in his book *The Great Hope of the Twentieth Century*, outlines processes of social transformation. He places technological progress at the heart of his argument: 'This [progress] drives up productivity and thus becomes the source of social wealth. As wealth increases, need structures and thus consumer preferences shift towards luxury goods and services. The production of services is largely resistant to technological progress and thus to productivity gains. This means that an ever-increasing proportion of the workforce is required to work in the service sector. Technological progress and changes in consumer preferences thereby lead to structural changes to the employment system, in the direction of more highly skilled and less onerous work in service sector jobs, to changes in people's

---

[40] *Clark*, Colin 1940: *The Conditions of Economic Progress*.
[41] Häußermann, Hartmut / Siebel, Walter 1995: *Dienstleistungsgesellschaften [Service Economies]*, p. 24.
[42] Bernd Bienzeisler: *Rationalisierung im Dienstleistungssektor – Strategien und Probleme [Rationalisation in the Service Sector - Strategies and Problems]*, p. 3.
[43] Fourastié, Jean 1954: *Die große Hoffnung des zwanzigsten Jahrhunderts [The Great Hope of the Twentieth Century]*.

lifestyles, in the direction of human urbanisation, and to changes in need structures, in the direction of *higher* demand. The growth of consumption-related services due to increasing consumer demand is the key driver of change.'[44] The insatiable 'hunger for the tertiary' (Fourastié 1954: 247) eventually results in around 80% of all workers being employed in the tertiary sector (which is characterised by limited increases in productivity) by the end of the transformation process. Fourastié sees this process lasting around 200-300 years. Only 10% of employment will then be accounted for by each of the first two sectors; all employment problems will be solved and a new quality of human coexistence will become possible.([45])

This, however, was a miscalculation. As the standard of living rises, there is indeed an increase in demand for services such as travel, healthcare, wellness and all kinds of luxuries. Ageing populations mean care services have to be expanded. Ever more complex societal relations and increasing environmental damage necessitate additional services in the form of consultancy and organisation. A plethora of different media emerge. More and more marketing know-how is called for in order to sell goods. In order to keep up with the pace of economic change, employees have to undergo constant training. In the course of production rationalisation, service areas such as legal departments, transport services, cleaning and security, dunning etc., are outsourced from production.

The latter services, however, are not new. They are simply outsourced from existing production facilities. Higher grade services remain in-country, while production is often relocated to low-cost countries. This outsourcing in conjunction with the relocation of production also increases the service intensity in the industrialised nations; in other words, the outsourcing of services also spells deindustrialisation.

But an increase in services does not mean services cannot be rationalised. On the contrary, as a consequence of computerisation and automation, right through to the use of robots, the service sector experiences at least as many job losses as industry, except

---

[44] Cited in Häußermann, Hartmut / Siebel, Walter 1995: *Dienstleistungsgesellschaften [Service Economies]*, p. 36.
[45] Bernd Bienzeisler: loc. cit., p.4.

where very unique roles are concerned. The number of people working as secretaries, bank employees, salespeople, telephone operators etc. steadily decreases as their roles are taken over by computers, machines and self-service facilities.'[46]

'Following the example of Ronald Reagan (in the USA) and Margaret Thatcher (in Britain), the CDU/FDP coalition under Helmut Kohl also pursued a supply-side economic policy. In accordance with this policy, the solution to unemployment as a consequence of accelerated economic growth was thought to be to increase corporate profits through tax cuts and deregulation.'[47]

As is illustrated by the following table, it was possible to cut the inflation rate with increased unemployment in Germany too. The tendencies towards rising unemployment and falling growth rates show, however, that the economy is in a state of secular stagnation.

---

[46] Taken from Uwe Petersen: *Wirtschaftsethik und Wirtschaftspolitik. Zur Überwindung der globalen Wirtschaftskrise. Von der liberalen zur sozialliberalen Wirtschaftsordnung [Economc Ethics and Economic Policy. On Overcoming the Global Economic Crisis. From the Liberal to the Social-Liberal Economic Order]*, Verlag Dr. Kovac Hamburg 2010, p. 200ff. A more detailed discussion can also be found there.

[47] Taken from Uwe Petersen as above, p.203

Indicators of economic development in West Germany 1982-1988 [48], from 1991[49], foreign trade balances from 1982[50]

Year	Inflation rate	Economic growth	Unemployment rate	Foreign trade balance
1982	5.3	1.1	7.5	+ 26 218
1983	3.3	1.9	9.1	+ 21 520
1984	2.4	3.1	9.1	+ 27 592
1985	2.2	1.8	9.3	+ 37 505
1986	-0.2	2.2	8.9	+ 57 581
1987	0.2	1.5	8.7	+ 60 198
1988	1.2	3.7	7.9	+ 65 468
1991	3.7		(West) 6.2	+ 11 197
1997	1.9	1.7	(West) 10.8	+ 59 548
2001	2.0	1.5	(West) 8.0)	+ 95 494
2005	1.6	0.7	(West) 11.0	+ 158 179
2012	2.0	0.7	(West) 5.9	+ 189 841

---

[48] Quoted from: Werner Zohlnhöfer and Reimut Zohlnhöfer: *Die Wirtschaftspolitik der Ära Kohl 1982–1989/90. Eine Wende im Zeichen der Sozialen Marktwirtschaft?[The Economic Policy of the Kohl Era 1982-1989/90. A Turning Point in the Nature of the Social Market Economy?]* With reference to: Sources: Federal Statistical Office (Unemployment rate; economic growth); OECD (inflation rate, investment rate).

[49]Inflation rates: http://de.statista.com/statistik/daten/studie/1046/umfrage/inflationsrate-ver-aenderung-des-verbraucherpreisindexes-zum-vorjahr/; Growth from 1991 onwards: http://de.statista.com/statistik/daten/studie/2112/umfrage/veraenderung-des-bruttoinlandpro-dukts-im-vergleich-zum-vorjahr/; Development of unemployment: http://de.wikipedia.org/wiki/Arbeitslosenstatistik.

[50] https://www.destatis.de/DE/ZahlenFakten/GesamtwirtschaftUmwelt/Aussenhandel/Gesamtentwicklung/Tabellen/GesamtentwicklungAussenhandel.pdf;jsessionid=A4420E1DA7A817C21D42BB18403C1AF9.cae3?__blob=publicationFile

Due to its high, and increasing, export surpluses, employment in Germany is higher than in many other countries. At the same time, however, these export surpluses are compensating for a lack of domestic demand. German savings in excess of investments are passed on to foreign countries in an amount equivalent to the export surpluses. They are returned in the form of demand from these foreign countries. In other words, without its export surpluses, the German economy would have collapsed.

4. The financialisation of the economy, and how it has degenerated into a casino

Economic activity is the procurement and distribution of scarce goods. Humankind is economically active in order to satisfy its needs. A need might also take the form of owning a castle, a yacht, works of art or treasures. And once money was invented, human beings also aspired to have as much of that as they could, particularly for times of need or major acquisitions.

Initially, money was also a good made from a precious metal, and thus had a value in and of itself. As gold increasingly failed to meet the liquidity needs of the growing economy, it was supplemented, and eventually largely replaced, by paper money.

Lending money in order to earn interest was something only usurers and pawnbrokers did, and was seen as immoral. This continued to be the case until loans were no longer granted primarily for consumption purposes but for investments. The interest was then a share of the profit, so to speak, which it was hoped the investments would generate.

For the setting up of large firms it proved useful to split ownership of the company up into part ownership and to issue documents confirming this ownership. This was how shares came into being. Shares could be traded, and a capital market arose for this purpose. So over and above real buying and selling activities, a new level of activity developed: that of buying and selling ownership titles.

Shares are issued in nominal amounts which express a certain share in the financing of the company. According to the estimated value of future dividends, shares are traded at a higher or lower price than the nominal value, meaning that the emissary or later the seller of shares can - or must - make capital gains, or capital losses. Because investments can go wrong, the risk of loss is built into the interest rate.

At first, investors tended to see themselves as co-owners of companies, and shares tended to reflect the asset value of the company: its machinery, its real estate, etc. But the more shares, corporate bonds and government bonds were traded on the capital market, the stronger the guild of the stockjobbers became. Stockjobbers were interested only in the monetary value of a capital market instrument. The purchase of shares came to be viewed less and less as a long-term investment in a firm. Instead, all anyone wanted to know was how soon they would see a return on their investment, and how much revenue it would generate. This meant investors were more interested in a company's *cash flow* than in its profits.

The next step was a growing detachment from the asset values of companies, and a situation where investors were no longer interested in anything but rates of return. Anything thought to be an asset value which was not absolutely essential for production (or which it was not possible to lease, for example) was rooted out and sold.

This approach, so focused on short term monetary returns, had initially been the preserve of the stockjobbers, but now began to take hold of investors too. It was also a catalyst for the establishment of so-called *hedge funds*. In accordance with the 'shareholder value principle', shareholders also obligated the directors of corporations to strive not to much to ensure the long-term success of the company as to maximise the short-term share price.

To this end, corporation directors were offered the prospect of generous bonuses and extra shares in their companies to appeal to their self-interest. As a consequence of this shareholder value corporate policy, the incomes of directors, compared with those on the lowest wages and salaries, rose to levels that were morally indefensible in relation to actual work done.

In this way the economy degenerated into a *casino* with a real economy attached. Purchases and sales on the capital market, the shifting of assets acquired from shares into other shares, parts of shareholdings and commodity funds, government bonds, currencies and, eventually, the bets that were placed on them, generated a liquidity requirement far exceeding the liquidity requirement for real economic transactions.

Central banks had to meet this need for liquidity by continually expanding the money supply, in order to avoid stifling the capital market and with it the real economy. This was because, given that more and quicker profits can be made on the capital market than can be made through productive work and manufacturing, banks only pass on credit to the real economy once the liquidity requirements of the capital market have been met. If the money supply were to be expanded on such a scale for real economic transactions alone, we would already be seeing runaway inflation. As it was, all that happened was more capital market speculation and an increase in the prices of shares and stocks such as real estate, artworks, gold etc. These price increases, however, are not classed as inflation.

As long as there exist an economy with a developed exchange of goods, as long also money exists. But money only used to have an auxiliary function in relation to real economic processes. As real economic objectives and behaviour fade into the background, however, giving way to monetary value optimisations and capital market transactions, the economy becomes *financialised*. The *financialisation* of the economy intensified, naturally, with the growing stock of tradeable capital market instruments and deindustrialisation.

Financialisation was even seen as an alternative to deindustrialisation. In fact, the Anglo-Saxon view was that a service economy - and particularly a financial-services-based economy - actually constituted an advanced stage of development in comparison to an industrial economy. For this reason, as outlined above, the British prime minister Margaret Thatcher (1979-1990) and the American president Ronald Reagan (1981-1989) encouraged deindustrialisation and particularly the concentration of financial services in their respective countries.

Reagan even believed that his so-called *supply-side*, ultimately capital-based economic policies would enable him to stimulate investment using tax cuts. Because the economy was still in a state of increasingly severe secular stagnation, however, this was doomed to fail. In the end, he ensured sufficient purchasing power through an enormous increase in debt-financed state spending. He also used tax cuts to promote capital market transactions and speculation. The tax savings, due to a lack of real economic investment opportunities, naturally led to an increase in investment-seeking speculative capital.

With Margaret Thatcher and Reagan (if not before) stagflation morphed into the *financialised* economy: an economic state in which not only are excess economic savings siphoned off by growing government debt and fed back into the real economic market as demand via state spending, but in which more and more capital is also burned on the capital market. As a result of the growing pressure to invest, investors pounced ever more recklessly on dubious investment opportunities which they were conned into by profit-hungry financial services providers. This led to the emergence in 1997 of the dotcom speculative bubble, during which, along with internet innovations, all sorts of other purportedly profitable *start-ups* were propagated and believed in. In turn, when the dotcom speculative bubble burst in 2000, a great deal of capital was burned.

Economic policy attempted to soften the blow of the emerging depression. Wikipedia stated: 'The US Federal Reserve is responding to the crisis, distributing money to banks at very low interest rates in order to pump liquidity into the financial markets. Following the stock market slump, new investment opportunities are being sought. The cheap money from the Federal Reserve is leading to increasing numbers of loans being granted to borrowers, including borrowers with lower and lower credit ratings ('subprime loans'). Creditworthiness checks are disappearing. US banks are issuing consumers with credit cards with low interest rate conditions.'[51]

Because a large proportion of excess savings worldwide were tied up in speculation, all the investors that were affected suffered considerable losses when the speculative bubble burst in 2007.

---

[51] http://de.wikipedia.org/wiki/Finanzkrise_ab_2007

III. The economic development of Japan as a model case of capitalist secular stagnation[52]

Until America forced Japan to open up to international trade in 1854, the Japanese economy had been guild-based, resembling economies in Europe in the Middle Ages. Japanese people were hardworking and aspired to wealth. But in pre-capitalist societies, people produced only as much as was needed for consumption and, where supplies for the future were concerned, only as much as could be stored in the form of goods or valuables.

After Japan opened up to the West, however, it wanted to adopt Western achievements as quickly as possible, partly in order to strengthen its independence and international position. In this way, Japan became the first industrial power in Asia. Japanese people retained their thrifty habits from pre-industrial times, however. This meant that the savings rate in Japan was traditionally high, and tended to be higher than in the other industrialised nations. As the table on Page 18f. illustrates, the savings rate in Japan in the years from 1955 to 1995 was between 12% and 24%, comparable with that of France, and even after that time it remained higher than in countries like the USA, Britain and Germany.

The high savings rate undoubtedly aided the formation of real capital and thus the industrial development of Japan. This resulted, however, in Japan's consumption lagging behind its production capacity. The demand gap was filled by military armament during the early period of Japan's industrial development - this was undoubtedly expedited by the helplessness Japan had experienced when it was forcibly opened up to the rest of the world. The pursuit of military power evolved into imperialistic policies, encouraged by the fact that Japan was lacking in raw materials and wanted to tap new sources of raw materials from outside the country.

---

[52] Mainly taken from: Uwe Petersen: *Die wirtschaftliche Krankengeschichte Japans [Japan's Economic Case History]*, in: *Unkonventionelle Betrachtungsweisen zur Wirtschaftskrise II. Krankheiten des Wirtschaftssystems und Möglichkeiten und Grenzen ihrer Heilung [Unconventional Views on the Economic Crisis II. Diseases of the Economic System and Limitations to its Cure]*, p. 122ff.

In this respect the militarisation of Japanese politics resembled that of Nazi Germany, which wanted to annex Eastern European countries under the motto 'Volk ohne Raum' ('People without space'). For the Japanese, as for the Nazis, the imagined supermacy of their own race served as a justification for their imperialism. They began to subjugate East Asia.

Another aspect of this imperialism was the fact that the Japanese made any savings they did not use for real investments available to the Japanese government for its militarisation programme, by buying Japanese government bonds. In this way Japan's public debt was funded, and still is to this day, largely by Japanese people.

If we take the criteria outlined earlier as a basis, we can see that the Japanese economy was suffering from secular stagnation from the very beginning, and that this secular stagnation was only prevented from becoming virulent by the fact that Japanese state spending absorbed all the country's excess savings capital.

After the second world war, Japan was forced to curb its military spending. Economic savings, therefore, were no longer needed for this purpose. At the same time Japan, like Germany, was able to acquire the latest technological know-how from the USA after the war, and experienced rapid economic development. But the consumer spending and investment made possible by the growth in incomes still lagged behind productive capacity.

Due to the cutbacks in spending on armaments, the savings that were not invested had to be offset by expanding export surpluses, and capital had to be exported accordingly. This turned Japan into the world's largest creditor. But export surpluses in relation to the USA alone reached such a level that the USA forced Japan to dismantle its direct, non-tariff import restrictions. In particular, the USA forced 'an appreciation of the yen in relation to the dollar which no longer corresponded to economic reality. This led to a reduction in the volume of Japanese exports.'[53] This did not lessen the pressure to invest, however.

---

[53] Wirtschaftskrise in Japan, *'Die wirkliche Krise kommt noch'* [Economic Crisis in Japan, *'The Real Crisis is Still to Come']*, in: *Das Weiße Pferd [The White Horse]*, Issue 14/98

Alongside a high-performing industrial sector, Japan has many traditional economic sectors and a particularly large number of smallholders. Germany Trade & Invest writes: 'The Japanese economy is marked by a clear dualism, with some large, internationally active and export-oriented companies and many small and medium-sized companies, which primarily target the domestic market. The big companies often play a pioneering role where technology is concerned. Small and medium-sized companies play an important role in terms of employment; however, this category of companies is currently nothing like as significant in terms of the country's economic and social development as it is in Germany. While big companies benefit from the weak yen and the growth in exports, many smaller and medium-sized companies are unable to pass on the increasing costs of their raw materials to consumers.'[54]

'The primary sector accounts for 1.4% of gross domestic product. There are still around 5% of workers employed in this sector, primarily in agriculture, which is heavily subsidised. This figure is well below the level of other developed economies.'[55]

This structure was, of course, one target of the USA's demand that these sectors be opened up to international competition. But when small-scale agriculture is exposed to competition from the large-scale agricultural production of North America, it risks being destroyed.

A free international market economy requires everyone to play to their own strengths, which also means that a less efficient system of agricultural production must be abandoned. This, however, is precisely where the limitations of the market become clear. Agriculture is also about the preservation of the countryside, and cannot simply be sacrificed in the name of the international division of labour. Furthermore, the entire population of Japan cannot become industrial workers - that would only add to the export surplus.

---

[54] Germany Trade & Invest: *Wirtschaftsentwicklung Japan 2007 [Economic Development in Japan 2007]*, 27/05/2008
[55] Germany Trade & Invest

And so, as a consequence of what one might call the *second forced opening of Japan's markets by the USA*, unemployment in the country rose. Unemployment leads to falling wages, or at least rules out any wage increases, even if industrial productivity - partly due to the drop in wages - rises.

This causes the distribution of income to shift even further in favour of the rich. The result is usually an increase in the savings rate. Experience has shown that in Japan the propensity to save increases under difficult working conditions. This led to a general increase in the pressure to invest, and this pressure found an additional outlet - a replacement, as it were, for the reduced capital exports - in Japanese real estate.

Das weiße Pferd notes: 'The economy still craved the drug of growth. A 'soap-bubble economy' emerged. Companies raised funds by taking out mortgages on their properties. With these funds they bought more property, which they used to borrow more money. Japanese property prices, already high, now rose to colossal levels. Even more money could now raised, and it funded even more speculation - in real estate, in shares, in foreign holdings. All without any real value.'[56]

The collapse of the speculative bubble in 1992 'left Japanese banks unable to collect outstanding receivables from loans to the tune of a colossal one billion marks. ... The collapse of the country's fourth biggest investment firm, Yamaichi, last October [1997] was not an isolated case: in recent years, three more brokerage houses and 22 banks went under. In most cases the state - in other words, the taxpayer - steps in and covers the losses. The profits that have been made through speculation are untouched: the losses are paid for by society.'[57]

As the Japanese ambassador reported: 'In the 1990s we experienced the collapse of the bubble economy in Japan, and following that a period of economic recession which is also known as the 'lost decade'. ... Around 86.7 billion Euros (approximately 10.4 trillion yen) of public funds was spent from 1996 to 2002 in order to guarantee savings deposits. And for the bad loans, around 80.8

---

[56] Wirtschaftskrise in Japan, *'Die wirkliche Krise kommt noch'* [Economic Crisis in Japan, *'The Real Crisis is Still to Come'*]
[57] loc. cit.

billion Euros (approximately 9.7 trillion yen) was used to buy up these loans from 1996 to 2005. As far as the nationalisation of banks was concerned, the Long-Term Credit Bank of Japan and the Nippon Credit Bank were both temporarily nationalised. In order to do this, a total of around 103.3 billion Euros (approx. 12.4 trillion yen) was spent from 1998 to 2006. Steps were taken to boost the economy in April 1998, in November 1998, in November 1999, in October 2000 and in April 2001; almost every year saw economic stimulus packages worth several trillion yen adopted and implemented.'[58]

These measures, which have continued to be implemented to this day and which have been reflected in ever expanding public debt, did succeed in mitigating the economic difficulties but not in solving the actual economic problem. As early as 1998, *Das weiße Pferd* observed: 'This problem has still not been dealt with.'[59] The same is still true today. In this respect, the Japanese real estate crisis of 1992 acts as a model for subsequent real estate crises including the one in the USA.

But while in Japan the pressure to invest was addressed as the real cause as early as 1998, and has been discussed as such ever since, until now it has been given little serious consideration in Europe, and still less in the USA. Back in 1998, *Das weiße Pferd* asked: 'Was it just excessive recklessness that caused the banks to give loans to anyone and everyone during the boom? Or does the problem actually lie in the fact that every bank nowadays needs to be able to recruit enough debtors for the ever growing amount of interest-requiring funds?'[60]

From 1998 onwards the debate around inequalities, particularly in relation to the development of income and wealth, began to intensify in Japan. 'In February 2006, prime minister *Koizumi* answered questions in parliament about inequalities in income and

---

[58] Japanese ambassador to Germany: *Die Internationale Finanz- und Wirtschaftskrise: Japans Beitrag zum Krisenmanagement. [The International Financial and Economic Crisis: Japan's Contribution to Crisis Management.]*

[59] Wirtschaftskrise in Japan, *'Die wirkliche Krise kommt noch'* [Economic Crisis in Japan, *'The Real Crisis is Still to Come']*.

[60] Wirtschaftskrise in Japan [Economic Crisis in Japan], loc. cit.

assets. In July the *Cabinet Office* published its *Annual Report on the Japanese Economy and Public Finance 2006*, in which the problem was addressed and analysed. ...

Public opinion surveys showed that subjective perceptions of inequalities are becoming more prevalent. In the *OECD Economic Survey of Japan 2006* it was pointed out that the Gini coefficient[61] has now risen above the OECD average, making the level of relative poverty in Japan one of the highest in any of the OECD nations.[62] Economists involved in the debate included Professor *Toshiaki Tachibanaki* from *Kyoto University*, who published *Nihon no keizai kakusa* [*Economic Inequality in Japan*] in 1998 and *Kakusa shakai - nani ga mondai nano ka* [*Social Inequality - the Essence of the Problem*] in 2006, and Professor *Fumio Ohtake* from *Osaka University*, whose essay *Nihon no fubyodo - kakusa shakai no genso to mirai* [*Divergences in Japan: Vision and Future of an Unequal Society*] appeared in 2005. ...

Public opinion surveys point overwhelmingly to the conclusion that a stronger perception of differences and inequalities has developed among the Japanese.[63] This is true of the increasing number of households which, as a result of corporate restructuring and job cuts, are faced with the prospect of irregular employment for their breadwinners. The growing number of 'freeters' and NEETs[64]

---

[61] The Gini coefficient is a numerical indicator of inequality measuring the extent to which the distribution of income deviates from a perfectly equal distribution. 0 represents perfect equality and 100 represents complete inequality (Appendix, Table 3-4, *Annual Report on the Japanese Economy and Public Finance 2006*).

[62] The *Ministry of Internal Affairs and Communications* stated in November 2006 that Gini coefficients had been calculated on the basis of disposable income in the *National Survey of Family Income and Expenditure 2004*, and that Japan was ranked 12th out of the 24 OECD countries with which a comparison was possible.

[63] Appendix, Table 3-10, *Annual Report on the Japanese Economy and Public Finance 2006*

[64] 'Freeters' are young people from 15 to 34 who work in part-time or temporary jobs. 'NEETs' (people who are Not in Employment, Education or Training) belong to the same age group and are classed as unemployed.

is partly attributable to the difficult employment conditions for young adults. Economists are paying close attention to increasing inequalities in income - a key aspect of the debate.

The Gini coefficient, which is based on published statistics, confirms a gradual increase in income disparities since the 1980s. According to the Japanese government, this was mainly down to the growing number of households made up of elderly people. From 1999 onwards, however, the Gini coefficient demonstrated an unmistakeable upward trend among younger people. In future there will undoubtedly be calls for further measures to diversify employment patterns, and more attention will be paid to the problems experienced by young adults in relation to these patterns.'[65]

Despite this debate, however, no economic policy conclusions were drawn in Japan either, with the result that the impact of *secular stagnation* continues to be felt. Just like in Germany today, a single remedy is proposed time and time again: increase domestic consumption. According to *Das weiße Pferd*, Western voices are even calling for 'those who 'refuse to consume' to be made to spend money via inflation.'[66]. But where is this increase in consumption supposed to come from, when the distribution of income is continually shifting further and further in favour of the wealthiest? And we forget 'that for many people, capital reserves are their only form of pension scheme or insurance against unemployment.'[67]

The only thing left to hope for, then, is catastrophes which might trigger public and private spending. On this subject, *Das weiße Pferd* stated in 1998: 'Japan has no GDR to assimilate in order to 'kickstart' its economy, no Euro-project, no EU-style eastward enlargement, no armaments industry, which has proved elsewhere to be a very good way of using up surplus capital at public expense so that it does not put pressure on the rate of return.'[68] This has changed now, of course, with the Fukushima nuclear crisis. This is why the crisis has already begun to raise hopes of an economic

---

[65] *Zunehmende Debatte über Ungleichheiten [Growing Debate Around Inequalities]*, in: February 2007 Japanese Economy Division Economic Research Department JETRO, S.11 http://www.jetro.de/d/ws2006.pdf
[66] Economic Crisis in Japan, loc. cit.
[67] loc. cit.
[68] loc. cit.

recovery. But this recovery is accompanied, just as the costs of reunification were in Germany, by yet more government debt. This is consistent with the way Japan (like the USA) has made public debt and increases in the money supply - *financialisation*, in short - into an all-purpose weapon for stabilising the economy.

Japan benefits, however, from the fact that public debt is mainly held by the Japanese themselves. There is hardly any danger of insolvency due to foreigners not rescheduling public loans or not granting new ones, and the Japanese themselves are still too loyal to their own nation to bet against their own currency. What stable convertible currency would they want to change their money into anyway?

The Japanese currency is also less at risk than other currencies because Japan is still one of the largest creditors in the world. Curiously, the yen even threatened to appreciate when the Japanese retrieved funds held abroad as a consequence of the Fukushima disaster. This inevitably created demand for the yen. In Japan, then, the shift in income distribution in favour of the wealthy will be allowed to continue, with the most serious problems being mitigated by more government debt and *financialisation*, i.e. a money glut.

If Japan genuinely wanted to solve its structural economic problems, however, it would first need to be aware that the creditors of its own government debt actually live in Japan, and that Japan could therefore offset Japanese domestic debt using creditors' debits. This domestic debt consists of nothing more than empty securities anyway, because the money that was given to the government has long since been used up and, as part of a settlement on the grounds of a lack of capital, creditors usually have to forego their claims.

In summary, the following diagnosis can be issued for Japan: Japan is suffering from:
- *secular stagnation*, despite also having
- *chronic current account surpluses* and one of the highest levels of *government debt* as a proportion of gross domestic product in the world - which, together with the current account surpluses, is barely enough to compensate for excess Japanese savings - and, as a result of the money glut,

- the *financialisation* of the economy.

Japan is thus a classic case of the economic disease of *secular stagnation*, despite having an active current account balance and almost no inflation.

B. Why is the present capitalist secular stagnation not recognised by prevailing neoclassical economic theory?

Carla Neuhaus reports: 'Crisis? What crisis? That's the question Lisa Großmann and Felix Kersting are finding themselves asking more and more as they sit in lecture halls listening to their professors. "The financial crisis is hardly ever mentioned in our lectures," they say. ...

When the financial crisis broke out in the USA five years ago, many economists were surprised. Very few of them had predicted it. Critics believe this is partly due to the way economists are trained. No changes have been made to university syllabuses since the crisis, however. ... In Hamburg, Heidelberg and Mainz, students in the working group *Real World Economics* are campaigning for 'a variety of economic theories' to be taught.

In making their protest, the Germans are following the example of young people in America. At elite university Harvard, students have been making headlines since 2011 when they simply stood up and left the room in the middle of a lecture being given by Gregory Mankiw. Mankiw is one of the world's best known economics professors, and has previously acted as an advisor to George W. Bush, among others. His lectures, say his students, are too one-sided. Their criticism is that Mankiw concentrates too much on neoclassical economics. For decades, this theory has been at the core of what is taught to students of economics. ...

Neoclassical economics assumes that human beings always behave rationally. Advocates of this school of thought also believe in the self-healing power of the markets, which they think automatically regain their equilibrium following a shock. Critics reject this - and see the financial crisis as proof. For the economy only regained its equilibrium after 2008 once governments across the world had stepped in with billions in state aid. This is exactly what the law of the market should have rendered unnecessary: everything ought to have sorted itself out automatically.

Supporters of the students include German economist Heiner Flassbeck. He is seen by other economists as an outsider. "It's a scandal that there are so many economics faculties in Germany where only one theory is being taught," says Flassbeck. He thinks the students are absolutely right to rebel against the current regime. He believes there is a flaw in the system; economists who subscribe to non-mainstream views, he says, have no chance of getting a professorship at a German university. This is why nothing else is being taught.

Tim Adam, who teaching corporate finance at Berlin's Humboldt University, sees things differently. "Neoclassical economics is a core element of teaching and research, and should remain so," he says. "It gives the students the tools they need to understand what typically happens in the economy. Crises are exceptional circumstances." The fact that so few economists predicted the crisis, claims Adam, is not due to the failure of the prevailing theory. "Crises happen when lots of economic operators have made bad decisions," he says. "But it is difficult to predict when people will make mistakes. We only ever know that in hindsight."[69]

Why does the prevailing doctrine find it so difficult to recognise secular stagnation?

I. Individualistic ideology

According to neoclassical theory, human beings are essentially selfish and only ever act in their own interests. Work is effort, and consumption is, in the broadest sense, human beings' purpose in life. People only work in order to satisfy their needs as effectively as possible.

This ideology is derived from Darwinian theory, according to which the fittest survive and the weakest starve due to limited resources, or are unable to reproduce because females always mate with the strongest males.

Darwin's theory seeks to explain the development of species. Capitalist ideology, however, is concerned with the development

---

[69] Carla Neuhaus: *Die Leere der Ökonomie. Professoren ignorieren bei der Ausbildung die Finanzkrise noch immer. Studenten protestieren – und unterrichten sich selbst [The Economic Black Hole: Professors are still failing to teach about the financial crisis. Their students are protesting - and are teaching themselves]*, in: Der Tagesspiegel No. 21 918, 5/1/2014, p. 21.

of the individual. Why human beings operate within social structures is not explained by the capitalist doctrine, unless we assume that human beings recognise that they are reliant upon their fellow human beings and have collectively agreed on some form of *social contract* like the one posited by Rousseau. For if human beings were to act in an entirely asocial way, the only possible outcome would be a dog-eat-dog world, a war of everybody against everybody.

The most effective way of combining individual work with social benefit is via the capitalist doctrine of the market. It is assumed that the market will regulate the supply and demand of goods and services in such a way that everybody will be able to sell their own labour in order to meet their own needs. Out of selfishness, everybody will offer the services they are best at providing and, being in competition with others, will also sell these services at the lowest possible price.

What is considered in theory, but not enough in practice, is that the optimal alignment by the market of each individual's services with their share of national product only works on the level of so-called 'atomistic' competition. Over time, however, the starting conditions for individual participants in market activities constantly change, so that stronger or more talented people then earn more and, what is more, are able to use their extra income to acquire production facilities, thereby increasing their share in economic value creation still further.

To the extent that these increases in income are acquired in return for an individual's services, they may be compatible with the system. What is not compatible with the system, however, is the passing down of acquired wealth to an individual's heirs. When this happens, individuals accrue income for which they have not had to provide any services. Thus, from generation to generation, income disparities between individuals become ever more pronounced and change in accordance with the starting conditions of new participants in the economy.

The use of patented know-how is regulated in a way which is compatible with the system: patents expire after a certain period of time, after which the know-how can be used by everyone. There are also competition laws to prevent the monopolisation of the market and thus remove impediments to optimal price-setting within the market. What is lacking, however, as a tool to ensure equal opportunity, is an appropriate inheritance tax to prevent too great a discrepancy between income earners. This is why we are now seeing an extremely unequal distribution of wealth and therefore of income.

According to the quasi-biological view of human economic behaviour, the sole purpose of work is to acquire consumer goods. Consequently, work should really be measured in such a way that human beings only work as much as they need to to meet their needs. Houses, castles, jewellery, artworks etc. are also consumer goods, of course. In pre-industrial times, these were some of the ways in which wealth was created. All assets, including gold and other precious metals, had to be created as part of the real economy.

This changed with the invention of money, particularly paper money. From then on, savings could also be amassed in money, and not spent again as demands on national product in real economic terms.

This possibility, however, was not taken into account by capitalist theory. For capitalist ideology assumes that saving is tantamount to refraining from consumption, and that human beings are only prepared to do this when they can reinvest their savings profitably and when they value the resulting profit more highly than consumption. This would mean that all savings would inevitably turn into investments. There would therefore be no discrepancy between the supply and demand on the market for goods.

II. Inadequate theory of the development of the relationship between economic supply and economic demand

With regard to the relationship between economic supply and economic demand, neoclassical theory does not attach enough importance to:
- demand for economic market equilibrium
- income distribution for economic market equilibrium

- rationalisation investments leading to job cuts in relation to innovative product developments and expansion investments which create jobs.

According to the prevailing neoclassical ideology, a general imbalance of supply and demand on the market is impossible. Certain products may be supplied that consumers do not need, or do not need in such large quantities. When this happens, prices will fall until these products are sold. Correspondingly, other goods will be in short supply and the prices of these goods will then rise. This ensures that companies will always adjust the supply of their products to fit the realities of the market. This, naturally, is a continuous process.

Saturation, according to neoclassical ideology, is only possible in relation to specific products. People can only eat a limited amount of bread or potatoes, for example. In principle, however, human beings' need to consume is supposed to be insatiable. But people can only want to buy what they know exists, and so new products need to be well advertised. In this respect, adequate marketing is a prerequisite for growth. The companies which have developed the new products, however, will ensure that this marketing happens.

One question remains: When new products are supplied, where does the purchasing power to generate demand for these products come from? According to Say's Law, the additional purchasing power is created by the supply itself, because when new products are produced, demand for these products is automatically generated in the form of wages, salaries, capital assets, pensions etc.

Since companies are the ones who are responsible for investing in and marketing products, it is companies whom neoclassical supply-oriented economic policy believes it is particularly important to support. Supply-oriented economic policy was developed in the mid-1980s under Reagan in the USA and under Margaret Thatcher in Great Britain. It subsequently became the model for the economic policy of all the industrialised nations.

According to this ideology, stagnation can only be overcome by strengthening investment opportunities for companies and investors. To this end tax cuts were advocated, particularly for the highest earners, to enable them to invest more. Banks' ability to grant credit was deregulated and wage levels were brought down. General wage cuts were facilitated in the USA and in Britain by weakening the trade unions, and in Germany by providing various forms of wage subsidies in conjunction with reductions in unemployment benefit, which force employees to work even in precarious jobs for low wages.

If not all workers are employed this can only be due (according to supply-oriented economic ideology) to the fact that the wages of the groups in question are too high, and that this means precarious employment is not possible or that products are being imported from low-wage countries or that production capacity is being relocated to these countries. Supply-oriented economic policy does hope that the wage level in developing countries will rise over time and that at some point those on the lowest incomes across the world will also be paid higher wages. In effect, however, it pushes down the wage level in industrialised countries to the level found in developing countries, with significant social consequences for the industrialised countries whose overall economic structure does not allow for wages as low as those in developing countries. According to the maxims of total competition there is of course no alternative to this lowering of the wage level in the industrialised nations: the only question is whether we should allow globalisation to proceed so far that individual countries' income structures and social structures may be destroyed in the process.

The crucial thing, however, is that supply-oriented economic policy does not take into account:
- that consumption capacity can be increased, but that the potential to increase it lessens as development progresses, so that as income rises, more and more is saved as the growth of consumer demand slows.
- that according to Say's Law, purchasing power does increase in line with increasing supply, but that it depends who is acquiring this purchasing power.

  As we have seen, the rate of rationalisation investments, which lead to job losses, tends to be higher than the rate of investments in innovation and expansion. Rationalisation investments, however, turn wage income into corporate earnings and capital income: in other words, the additional income mainly falls to high earners, leading to a redistribution of income from earners with a high consumption rate to earners with a low consumption rate. For this reason, but also as a result of unequal income distribution, the volume of savings in the economy grows even more quickly, without there being any prospect of additional investments in innovation or expansion on an equivalent scale.

- The importance of state spending for balancing out supply and demand. In pre-capitalist times, demand from the nobility for weapons and luxuries shaped the development of production. Following the abolition of serfdom, labour dues were no longer levied on serfs. Instead the state acquired the means to finance its needs by taxing and borrowing.

When one looks at the factors in the economic development of the industrialised nations not just from a business perspective but also from the point of view of public spending, the importance of the latter in maintaining the equilibrium of the market economy becomes very clear. In Germany, the proportion of economic demand currently generated by the state stands at around 45%. Much of this is social spending - it accounts for 38.6% of the federal budget, or 50.5% taken together with spending on the healthcare system.[70] These large social transfers are the consequence of the one-way income shift in favour of employers and holders of capital over the course of economic development.

Public spending is not only largely independent of economic conditions but is even, as far as social spending is concerned, counter-cyclical - in other words, it rises when earnings fall or are lost altogether. Where social transfers are funded by insurance benefits, the economic savings rate drops accordingly; where they are funded by government debt, excess savings are siphoned off and fed back into economic demand. Since the introduction of general social insurance and employment incentive measures, therefore, consumer demand does not fall too dramatically even in the event of rationalisation investments, meaning that symptoms of stagnation can be easily overlooked.

---

[70] Report by Der Tagesspiegel No. 21872, 17/11/2013, p. 5. Source: Federal Ministry of Finance

Although a savings rate in excess of real economic investment opportunities would be bound to rise even higher in the event of tax cuts, supply-oriented economic policy lowered taxes even for higher earners, as is shown in the table below by figures from four countries representative of the trend.

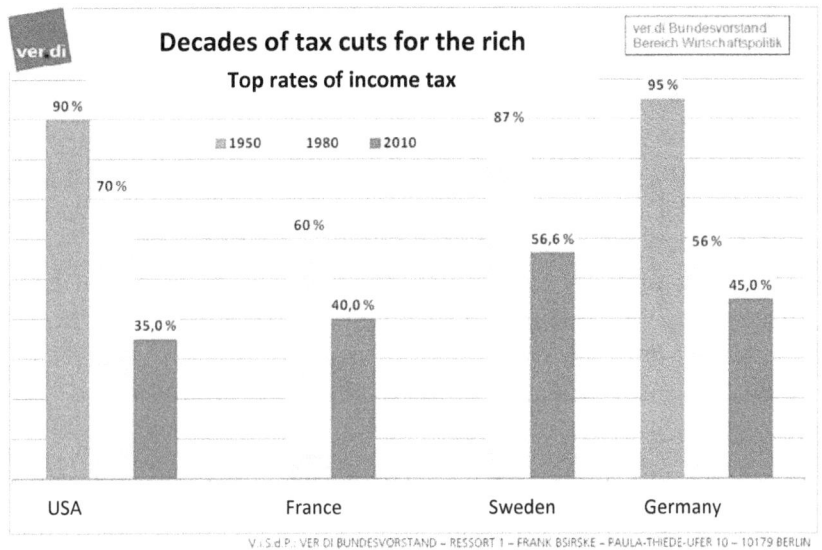

It could not be clearer how little understanding the prevailing economic doctrine has of secular stagnation.

If the causes of secular stagnation were properly understood, then we would act upon the ideas of Nobel Prize winner *Paul Krugman*, as the *Deutsche Mittelstands Nachrichten* explains. 'He wants to raise income tax to 91%, and says this is only fair and the only way to ensure growth.

The success of the American economy after the Second World War shows that 'you can have prosperity without demeaning workers and coddling the rich', wrote Nobel Prize winner Paul Krugman in Sunday's New York Times. He waxes nostalgic about the 1950s. At that time the top rate of tax was 91%, and the trade unions were much more powerful than they are today. 'We can do that again,' says the influential economist. He believes rich people need to contribute their 'fair share' and that workers should be paid 'decent wages'. Only this, he claims, will ensure prosperity.

In the 1950s, the top rate of tax was 91% and taxes on corporate profits were twice as large, relative to gross domestic product, as they are today. 'Nor were high taxes the only burden wealthy businessmen had to bear,' Krugman adds. In those days, he says, strong trade unions wielded a degree of bargaining power that is difficult to imagine today. They bargained with managers as equals. These conditions led to economic growth from which everybody benefited, enthuses the economist - though the executives of the 1950s were 'relatively impoverished' by today's standards.

Today, things are very different. Now executives have mansions, 'armies of servants' and large yachts, writes Krugman critically. And anyone proposing political action against this situation 'is met with cries of "socialism".' Barack Obama's threat, during the run-up to the election, to 'modestly raise taxes on top incomes' was deemed harmful to the economy by his opponent. But the Nobel Prize winner vehemently contradicts the advocates of lower taxes.'[71]

These flawed tax reduction policies were also implemented in Germany; though in mitigation of individual countries' actions, it must be acknowledged that ruinous international competition forced them to combat an exodus of corporate management by lowering corporate taxes.

Margit Schratzenstaller writes: 'Corporation tax on retained profits, which had stood at 56% since 1977, had already been lowered to 50% in 1990 and then to 45% in 1994. In 1999 it was reduced to 40% (42% including solidarity surcharge), and in 2001 it fell to 25% (26.4% including solidarity surcharge). Corporation tax on distributed profits was cut to 30% in 1994, and in 2001 it was brought down to the same level as for retained earnings (26.4% including solidarity surcharge). At shareholder level, the half-income method was introduced.

The corporate tax cuts by the red-green coalition (the Social Democrats and the Green Party) ([72]), included other asset relief measures alongside a reduction in corporation tax. There was exemption from corporation tax and trade tax on profits from the sale

---

[71] Deutsche Mittelstands Nachrichten | 25/11/12, http://www.deutsche-mittelstands-nachrichten.de/2012/11/48396/

[72] For details see Bach 2001 or Schratzenstaller 2002

of shares by corporations and on dividend payments between corporations with substantial participation interests, and it was made easier for companies to form corporation and trade tax groups. Taxes on trading capital had already been abolished by the previous government in 1998 as part of the Company Tax Reform Continuation Law, turning trade tax into a largely income-related and thus much more cyclical tax. In 2008, corporation tax was reduced to its current level of 15%, and the trade tax base rate ([73]) was cut from 5% to 3.5%. This meant that the combined corporate tax rate (corporation tax on retained profits and general corporation tax including solidarity surcharge, plus trade tax) had been reduced from 60% at the end of the 1970s to 38.9% as of 2001 and around 30% as of 2008. The measures taken to widen the tax base (including the introduction of an interest barrier, depreciation restrictions, the widening of the trade tax base rate through various additions), only partially filled the funding gap that resulted from the revenue losses associated with the lowering of taxes.

In an entrepreneurial context, the top rate of income tax on business income, which applies to one-person companies and partnerships, is relevant. It was cut from 56% at the end of the 1970s to 47.5%, including solidarity surcharge (as of 2007), with a reduced top rate of tax on business income granted between 1994 and 2001. The 2008 corporate tax reform introduced a reduced rate of tax on retained profits, amounting to 28.25% (or 29.8% including solidarity surcharge). One-person companies and partnerships therefore pay the same rate of corporate tax on retained profits as a corporation, instead of a top tax rate of 47.5%. And if we consider that since 2001 one-person companies and partnerships have been able to completely offset trade tax, de facto, against income tax, ([74]) then the reduction in the tax rate on the profits of one-person companies and partnerships turns out to be just as significant as for corporation tax.'[75]

---

[73] Trading profits (after allowances have been deducted) are multiplied by the trade tax base rate to give the basis of assessment for trade tax.
[74] Through the introduction in 2001 of a crediting factor for trade tax to income tax of 1.8, which was raised to 3.8 in 2008.
[75] Margit Schratzenstaller: Für einen produktiven und solide finanzierten Staat Determinanten der Entwicklung der Abgaben in Deutschland [For a

'With the tax reform of 2000 the top rate of income tax and the basic tax rate, among other things, were cut in several stages (...) The top rate of tax, which since the 1950s had stood at between 53% (until 1974 and from 1990 onwards) and 56% (from 1975 to 1989), was lowered to 42% by 2005. At the same time, between 2000 and 2004 the threshold for the top rate of income tax was lowered from 58,643 Euros to 52,151 Euros (it has since risen slightly to 52,882 Euros as of 2010). In 2007, an (additional) top tax rate of 45% was introduced for taxable annual incomes above 250,000 Euros (the so-called second proportional zone or 'tax on the rich'); this additional threshold for the top rate of income tax currently stands at 250,731 Euros.

The basic rate has also been cut in several increments by a considerable amount since the end of the 1990s. Until 1994 it had always stood at between 19% and 22%; for the period from 1995 to 1998 it had been raised to 25.9%. Between 1999 and 2005 it was incrementally reduced to 15%, and since 2009 has stood at 14%. Parallel to this, the basic tax-free allowance, which by 1996 had more than doubled (from 2,871 Euros to 6,184 Euros), was raised in yearly increments from 1998 to 2004 to 7,664 Euros, in order to comply with constitutional law. In 2009 and 2010 the allowance was increased again to 7,834 Euros and 8004 Euros. The tax cuts were partly funded by the restriction or complete abolition of tax credits (including various special payments for employees, home offices, private tax advice costs, homeowner subsidies and saver's allowances). Overall, however, private households saw significant reductions in terms of the income tax they paid.([76])

Along with the reduction of the standard rate of income taxation as part of the progressive income tax rate, the exclusion of capital

---

Productive and Solidly Financed State. Determinants of the Development of Spending in Germany]; Study commissioned by the Department of Economic and Social Policy at the Friedrich-Ebert Foundation, in: WISO Diskurs January 2013, p. 20.

[76] For a more detailed explanation and analysis see Seidel 2001: Seidel, B. 2001: *Die Einkommensteuerreform* [*The Income Tax Reform*], in: Truger, A. (ed.): Rot-grüne Steuerreformen in Deutschland. Eine Zwischenbilanz [Red-green Tax Reforms in Germany. An Interim Balance], Marburg, p.21 - 46

income from progressive income taxation in 2009 and the introduction of a proportional withholding tax of 25% also represent forms of tax relief.'[77]

Naturally, Germany too felt obliged to take part in the tax cut rally. To resist it, new initiatives are required to stem the ruinous tide of tax cutting. Through its tax cuts, Germany too has contributed to the weakening of economic demand.

At best, supply-side economic policies have helped to balance economic supply and demand by burning capital through gambling on the capital market, and through speculation. The fact that symptoms of the crisis, particularly in the USA, remained under control is mainly attributable to the incredibly rapid growth of public debt during the Reagan administration, which directed excess savings back into real economic circulation via state spending.

III. Lack of understanding of the role of money in a primarily capital-market-oriented economy

Capitalist ideology assumes that, because abstention from consumption is rare, savings are only offered in return for preferential rates of interest. The interest rate reflects the relative scarcity of savings, and the risk of losing the money is naturally factored into the interest rate.

As regards monetary policy, neoclassical economic theory assumes that economic upswings alternate with downturns and that central banks simply need to counteract extreme swings in the form of inflationary or deflationary developments by raising interest rates and restricting the money supply, or lowering interest rates and expanding the money supply. As a result, ups and downs in terms of interest rates and the money supply would then be compensated for, as long as the money supply does not have to increase because economic growth increases the liquidity requirement. Secular stagnation such as we have been experiencing since

---

[77] Margit Schratzenstaller loc. cit., p. 18f.

the end of the postwar reconstruction period, which has led to interest rates being at their lowest for years without a resulting surge in investment, does not feature in neoclassical economic theory. There is therefore no economic policy model to deal with it. In particular, what the theory fails to realise is that the majority of money is needed for capital market transactions and speculation.

As a result of speculation, the prices of shares, real estate, commodities etc. are driven ever higher. The liquidity requirement increases accordingly. If this increasing liquidity requirement is not taken into account by central banks, speculation collapses.

In order to combat depressive tendencies, central banks worldwide repeatedly lowered interest rates and flooded the economy with money. The same was true of the European Central Bank.

However, the legal framework for the European Central Bank's monetary policy is also regulated according to neoclassical economic policy. It is understandable, therefore, that one might have serious concerns about the unlimited purchase (if this is thought necessary) of Eurozone government securities by the ECB, and might see this as indirect, forbidden public finance. When the government securities that have been bought or are going to be bought come from crisis countries within the Eurozone, the ECB is also assuming the risks of devaluation, and these risks are thus ultimately borne by all the Member States of the Eurozone. In other words: by purchasing distressed securities, the ECB is placing a financial burden on the Member States and thereby also interfering with the budgetary powers of Member State parliaments.

When we find ourselves, contrary to neoclassical interpretations of economic problems, in a state of secular stagnation, and the outbreak of crises resulting from the increasing liquidisation of the economy and the insolvency of individual states, and thus the Euro, can only be prevented by the purchase of government bonds by the ECB, then the Eurozone would be doing itself a disservice if it were to sabotage ECB President Draghi, with his assurances that he will do everything in his power to rescue the Eurozone. Because, as Holger Zschäpitz reports from the latest Davos Conference: 'A good half of the economic elite now considers deflation to be a far greater risk for Europe than inflation, including the head of Deutsche Bank, Anshu Jain, Nobel Prize winner Joseph Stiglitz and economics professor Michael Porter.

One man thinks deflation is already just around the corner. 'The ECB needs to act now in order to keep us from tipping over the edge,' said Berkeley professor Barry Eichengreen in *Die Welt*. "Once we enter a downward spiral, it'll be too late."'[78]

In fact, Draghi's statement served to calm speculation against the ailing nations and the Eurozone as a whole. Because of the pressure to invest excess savings, Draghi even managed to enable Greece, which in and of itself is still very weak, to borrow on the capital market again. This was despite the fact that

- unemployment in Greece has reached a record high and
- the budget deficit represents 12.7% of gross domestic product (GDP), 'as the European statistics office Eurostat announced in Luxembourg on Wednesday [23/4/2014]' - even if 'the majority is accounted for by capital injections for Greek banks'[79] - meaning that
- public debt 'rose from 157.2% of GDP in 2012 to 175.1 % last year, by far the highest level of any of the European Member States.'[80]
- Gerd Höhler and Christopher Ziedler write: 'Many economists believe that Greece, even with lower interest rates and longer repayment terms, will not be able to escape from the debt trap and will instead need a drastic haircut on its debt.'[81]

---

[78] Holger Zschäpitz, Davos: *Deflationsgefahr. Geldhistoriker warnt vor fataler Abwärtsspirale [Deflation Risk. Economic Historian Warns of Fatal Downward Spiral].* DIE WELT 24/01/14,
http://www.welt.de/finanzen/article124170432/Geldhistoriker-warnt-vor-fataler-Abwaertsspirale.html

[79] Gerd Höhler and Christopher Ziedler: *Wacklige Angelegenheit. Griechenland vermeldet erstmals seit vielen Jahren wieder einen Einnahmenüberschuss – doch Zinsen sind dabei herausgerechnet. Ist die Euro-Krise überstanden? [A Shaky Business. Greece reports a revenue surplus for the first time in many years - but interest has been deducted. Have we overcome the Euro-crisis?]* in: DER TAGESSPIEGEL No.22025, 24/4/2014, p.2.

[80] Gerd Höhler and Christopher Ziedler: loc. cit.

[81] loc. cit.

Greece's ability to borrow again is being sold by economic policymakers as a sign that a highly-indebted Greece has regained the confidence of investors. What is actually giving investors confidence, however, is the fact that if necessary, the whole of the Eurozone, via the ECB, will guarantee the repayment of Greece's debts. The Central Bank's declaration makes all the countries in the Eurozone liable for Greece's debts, in a communitisation of debt which is deeply concerning from the point of view of both international and constitutional law.

Moreover, the Eurozone countries are also indirectly paying the increased interest rates that investors receive for new Greek bonds. Because, as a result of a shift from, for example, German debt instruments to Greek ones, the price of German securities may fall, so that at a later date Germany too may only be able to borrow at higher interest rates. If the European Central Bank is ultimately liable for Greek debts, and wants to give Greece the opportunity to borrow more, it would be better for the loans Greece needs to be given to it directly by the European Central Bank at favourable interest rates. Greece would be better served by his - and why should investors profit from the fact that Europe is liable for Greece?

'At the peak of the financial crisis in late 2011 and early 2012, the ECB had already flooded the financial system with two liquidity injections of at least 500 billion Euros each. At that time, however, the banks had invested a large part of the money in government bonds, seen as safe investments - which may have propped up states and banks, but did not lead to any new loans.' [82] Because the European Central Bank believes that in a thriving economy prices should rise by about 2% per year, it is afraid of prices falling even further and of ending up with deflation.

Because the ECB realised, however, that the money was not reaching the real economy but was merely boosting speculation on the capital market,

---

[82] http://www.tagesschau.de/wirtschaft/ezb-leitzins-100.html

- it is making all commercial banks pay a penalty interest rate if they park excess liquidity with the European Central Bank[83] and
- it only plans to supply commercial banks with Central Bank funds on a large scale if they pass these funds on to the real economy.

Monetary policy measures can influence speculation by investors; however, supply-oriented neoclassicists - and their ideology also dictates the ideology of the European Central Bank - are wrong in thinking that these measures can also be used to boost the real economy. For neoclassicists only ever argue in terms of supply: according to them, all cost reductions, and thus all interest rate reductions, must necessarily boost investment. Given that demand - particularly in the industrialised nations but also due to unequal income distribution amongst those with purchasing power - is largely sated, further reductions in interest rates cannot trigger any real economic investment, particularly given that interest rates are at a historic low.

But the European Central Bank still seems, like the majority of economic politicians, to want to tackle deflation in accordance with supply-oriented economic policy, and has evidently not realised that the cause is one of structural demand - i.e., that we are experiencing secular stagnation. In other words, the ECB is hoping, by its targeted granting of credit to commercial banks (to be passed on to the real economy) and by cutting interest rates yet again, to stimulate demand for consumer and capital goods.

As far as consumer demand is concerned, the ECB seems to be assuming that demand is essentially determined by price expectations. This means that deflation, or a downward spiral in prices, occurs, 'when consumers and investors believe that prices could soon fall even further and therefore postpone their spending.' [84] Conversely, then, one could conclude that demand would be stimu-

---

[83] so as not to endanger their solvency but also in order to comply with European Central Bank rules, commercial banks must comply with certain ratios of credit granted to cash reserves. For this reason, they are tending to take up the cheap loans provided by the Central Bank, but then to park all their free funds in their Central Bank account overnight.

[84] http://www.tagesschau.de/wirtschaft/ezb-leitzins-100.html

lated by inflationary price developments. Price development expectations are thus held responsible for economic growth, or the lack of it. A rather blinkered argument!

The expected alterations in price for individual products would have to be very large to cause citizens to bring forward or to postpone demand. Also, purchases that were brought forward, unless they involved food or travel, would not be made later on, and would therefore not reduce the overall demand gap in the medium-term.

A much more important deciding factor where economic demand is concerned is the development and distribution of purchasing power - in short, income distribution. Given the current distribution of income and the saturation level of individual income groups, the Central Bank cannot stimulate consumer demand by lowering interest rates. On the contrary; if interest rates for small savers are lowered, consumer demand may even drop. So where is the unsaturated consumer purchasing power in the industrialised nations - I do not say need, but purchasing power - for businesses to invest in? It is thus to be expected that the additional funds will not be sufficiently made use of or that they will simply be used to play the capital markets again.

The Association of Savings Banks and the German Insurance Association have been accordingly critical: "Instead of boosting the economy in crisis countries, as had been hoped, the new cut in interest rates has unsettled savers across Europe and destroyed the value of assets," said the president of the German Savings Bank and Giro Association, Georg Fahrenschon. Nor did the measures make the financial market any more stable - "on the contrary, the overabundance of money is already starting to seep out of every nook and cranny, seeking ever more risky investment opportunities. The German insurance industry also maintained that the decisions were "absolutely the wrong economic medicine to prescribe". "The low interest rates are hardly generating any growth impulses at all," said the president of the German Insurance Association, Alexander Erdland'.[85]

---

[85] http://www.tagesschau.de/wirtschaft/ezb-leitzins-100.html

Dirk Elsner even doubts whether the restrictions imposed by the Central Bank to get banks to pass on the additional credit to the real economy is actually working, and fears it might lead to "financing by 'shadow banks', criticised worldwide." Elsner explains: 'The term 'shadow banking system' denotes all sorts of activities and entities outside of the regulated banking system. According to the German Bundesbank (see 'The shadow banking system in the Eurozone', p. 18) the shadow banking system comprises all entities and activities involved in credit intermediation outside of the regular banking system. This is usually understood to refer to financing by special purpose vehicles, investment funds, hedge funds, private equity, pensions funds and insurers. In fact, however, according to the German Bundesbank's definition, loans between businesses are also classed as shadow banking.

According to the German Bundesbank, non-banks should not actually be given any access to Central Bank liquidity. But they are the very entities that do tend to access it as a result of the measures outlined above. The ECB is thereby contributing to the fragmentation of the financial system, shifting risks to the private sector and ending up with them on its own balance sheets. Companies are taking on more and more banking functions. And from the point of view of companies trying to obtain finance, supplier credit or investment financing from a parent company may well be much more attractive, quicker and less bureaucratic than finance from a bank.'[86]

What an even bigger supply of money and even lower interest rates might well encourage, however, is more playing of the capital market and more speculative bubbles. In this way capital is also burnt on the capital market.

Where government bonds are subscribed to, savings will turn back into economic demand via state spending. Property speculation, which not only raises the value of existing properties but also triggers new builds, becomes investment and, where rising asset

---

[86] Dirk Elsener: *Wie die neue EZB-Politik Schattenbanken fördert [How the ECB's New Policies are Encouraging Shadow Banking]*, in: THE WALL STREET JOURNAL, 20/6/2014
http://www.wsj.de/article/SB10001424052702304911804579635852014191932.html

values tempt people to consume more and spend more money on luxuries, is also burned as savings capital. The latter development also tempts earners on lower incomes and even those who are relatively impoverished to finance additional spending through consumer credit. In this way the expansion of the money supply and the lowering of interest rates also help to close the demand gap and prevent the outbreak of crises.

Expansionary monetary policy and interest rate cuts are most effective when extra government securities are also made available - i.e. when governments borrow more. This is still happening, because public expenditure in most countries is not financed by adequate public revenues. Because state spending is supposed to be being cut in order to reduce the public debt burden (debt brakes!), a brake is also put on the burning of capital via state spending, which inevitably heightens the global economy's vulnerability to crises. By neoclassicists, however, debt reductions are only ever classed as economic consolidation.

Economists like Larry Summers and Paul Krugman, who have already realised that the global economy is in a state of secular stagnation, are even hailing the encouragement of speculative bubbles as a solution to be adopted by future economic policy in periods of secular stagnation. Larry Summers argues as follows: 'Over the past 50 years, the Fed cut short-term interest rates during every recession in order to boost economic growth. Now interest rates are close to zero and the recovery is still anaemic. Savings are well in excess of investments.'[87]

Because, as has been shown, excess savings capital can be burned on the capital market, Summers comes to the conclusion that monetary policy should encourage speculative bubbles and thus help stabilise demand. Because with every crisis, wealth is destroyed. K. Singer writes: 'Summers' idea, according to which the world is in danger of descending into secular stagnation, was enthusiastically praised by Nobel Prize winner Krugman. In light of this

---

[87] K. Singer: Summers: Säkulare Stagnation [Secular Stagnation], http://www.timepatternanalysis.de/Blog/2013/11/21/summers-sakulare-stagnation/

danger, Summers touts asset price bubbles as being not only inevitable but desirable. And Krugman, the prize winner, cheers him on.'[88]

But it is also important to be aware of the dangers of an unchecked flood of money. Because with every additional banknote on the capital market, the potential for speculation in currencies grows. The more of a nation's money there is in circulation, the stronger the possibility that the currency will be speculated against and that the currency exchange rate will plummet. Large countries like the USA, but also the Eurozone, are less at risk of this happening.

Central banks are hoping that their flood of money will facilitate real economic actions. In practice, however, its chief effect has been to stimulate capital market speculation. When the potential for price increases on shares, gold or anything else is exhausted and investors switch to profit-taking, the next crisis is unleashed.

In addition, the economy's potential for incurring debt increases. Because money creation is also always linked to a corresponding level of debt, which is compensated for at the banks through the collection of assets. Thus a central bank receives the equivalent value of the money it has issued in gold or securities, and this also applies to loans from commercial banks to non-banks. If the value of these securities falls in relation to the value of the money issued, and if borrowers cannot make up the difference between the credit and the security provided, then bankruptcies may occur, and this may also trigger an economic crisis.

Due to the central banks' cuts in interest rates, investors, and particularly speculators, are able to refinance at exceptionally favourable terms. In this way, investors and speculators profit from low interest rates at the expense of savers. As long as interest rates on savings are lower than the rate of inflation, savers are even expropriated in favour of investors and speculators.

This is why investment consultants advise capital investors to buy shares instead of saving. As experience has shown, this advice is only applicable to small investors when the share price is low. But when the share price has been pushed up by general pressure

---

[88] K. Singer: *Blasen her! [Bring on the Bubbles!]* Source: http://www.timepatternanalysis.de/Blog/2013/11/27/blasen-her/

to invest and by high profit expectations, influenced by speculation, small investors only ever stand to lose, because the share price is bound to collapse sooner or later particularly due to the fragility of the economy in periods of secular stagnation. Large investors can get over the resulting losses of assets, unless they are heavily in debt and are no longer able to repay their loans. Small investors, however, can lose all of their assets and their entire pension.

Whenever investors are encouraged by the availability of cheap money to buy property, and this property increases in value as a result of the increase in demand, property owners will pass rising costs on to renters. This leads to an increase in incomes earned from rents and leases, at the expense of the purchasing power of renters, which means another shift in income distribution in favour of a smaller number of earners. These dangers are naturally exacerbated by central banks cutting interest rates below zero. The latest interest rate cuts and the announcement of extra central bank loans to commercial banks to be passed on to the real economy, as well as interest rates on commercial bank deposits with the ECB, are considered by the 'markets', after the model of the famous Krupp cannon, as a particularly effective means of stimulating the economy, or at least the capital market. The DAX promptly reached 'the 10,000 point mark for the first time in response to the ECB's Big Bertha.'[89]

The central banks, by buying up government bonds on the capital market in a targeted manner, or by threatening to do so, can also exert a controlling influence on and thus regulate the speculative behaviour of investors. Central Bank president Mario Draghi's announcement that the ECB would do "whatever it took" to save the euro was enough to end the speculation against the euro, in 2012.

As a consequence of the ECB's latest decisions, interest rates on government bonds fell accordingly. 'The decline was particularly pronounced on the bonds of Eurozone countries weakened by the crisis, which stood to profit most from the ECB aid. In France,

---

[89] http://www.wiwo.de/finanzen/geldanlage/nach-ezb-zinssenkung-richtig-mischen-an-der-boerse/10001620-2.html

which is now seen as the biggest 'problem child', interest rates also fell. There, the yield on ten-year debt instruments fell to a record low.

The steepest drop was in interest on securities with five-year maturities. In Greece, the yield on five-year government bonds fell by almost half a percentage point in one afternoon, to 4.24%. In Italy and Spain there were declines of around a quarter of a percentage point, and yields fell to 1.3% and 1.12% respectively. Interest rates also fell by a significant amount in Portugal and Ireland.[90]

The fact that investors are content to accept such low interest rates on government bonds with no material value, the repayment of which is only ensured by the ECB's virtual guarantee, and which still come with an obvious price risk, is in turn evidence of the enormous pressure to invest which is a typical sign of secular stagnation.

Although the central banks' low interest rate policy and money glut are encouraging investors to play the capital market and destroying the economy in the long term, they are, to some extent, managing to prevent the outbreak of economic crises in the short term. This was why the Fed, to prevent the property market in the USA collapsing through lack of funds, pumped more and more money into it, and why commercial banks were also encouraged by deregulation to expand their own money creation. Consequently we still have - or have again ended up with - a growing liquidity supply, in order to stop the capital market from collapsing and endangering the borrowing requirements of the real economy.

IV. Inadequate theory of economic growth

Today, the health of an economy is measured in levels of growth. A high level of economic growth is classed as healthy, a stagnating or shrinking economy as unhealthy. This assessment is not self-evident, however. Because, as was noted earlier, ancient cultures

---

[90] http://www.t-online.de/wirtschaft/boerse/anleihen/id_69751424/europas-anleihezinsen-nach-ezb-lockerung-auf-talfahrt.html

remained at the same stage of development in terms of their civilisation and culture, using traditional goods and means of production, for millennia, yet they were not seen as unhealthy.

In principle it is possible, even with the highly developed productive forces we have today, to imagine economic orders in which we only produce as much as is needed, given a certain standard of consumer goods, to meet people's needs. When we consider that invested sums could be written off and that in an amount equivalent to these write-offs, more productive assets could be acquired, then an economy could even grow without having to refrain from consumption, or working hours could be reduced to enable people to have more free time.

The reason *economic growth* is now used as a measure of economic health has less to do with people's needs than with the necessity that savings be invested and the fact that they need to be fed back into economic demand if the economic balance of demand and supply is not to be destroyed.

In the past, excess revenues led to material wealth in the form of gold, land, castles, cultural monuments etc. This enabled nobles, Indian maharajahs and other elites of the past to amass immeasurable treasures and at the same time to promote culture; and yet these economies were not seen as unhealthy, even though the lower classes were forced to live in wretched poverty. Today, savings are not used predominantly to increase external wealth. Nowadays savings are supposed to be invested, in order to generate more profit, and this profit need no longer bear any relation to the material needs of the investor.

Moreover, the aim is no longer a *reasonable* amount of profit, or an amount *befitting one's social status*. Now, everything is about *maximum* profit. Economies must grow in order to generate new profit opportunities for savings[91], and if the economies do not grow, they collapse.

---

[91] For more detail see: *Warum muss eine Wirtschaft wachsen? [Why Does an Economy Have to Grow?]*, in: Uwe Petersen: Unkonventionelle Betrachtungsweisen zur Wirtschaftskrise: Von Haien, Heuschrecken und anderem Getier. [Unconventional Views on the Economic Crisis: On Sharks, Locusts and Other Animals]. Verlag Peter Lang 2011, p. 27ff.

Because all profit opportunities, however, are ultimately dependent upon the development of consumer demand, it becomes clear that economic demand still plays a crucial role. When economic demand is non-existent and cannot be stimulated, partly because the majority of the population does not have sufficient purchasing power at their disposal as a result of unequal income distribution, and the rich have consumed as much as they want already, then the economy must shrink until all savings as investments have been turned back into economic demand.

The hypothesis according to which 'in the long term, the capitalist economic system will enter a stationary state devoid of economic growth', was already being advanced many years ago by Keynes, and particularly Hansen. According to this hypothesis, secular stagnation arises 'in situations of relatively high per capita income, where an excessive average savings rate leads planned savings to exceed planned investments. This sets off a long-term process of contraction, which does not stop until a low enough national level of income is reached for planned saving and planned investment to balance each other out again. The economy then remains at this level.'[92]

One objection to this argument, as outlined in *Gablers Wirtschaftslexikon [Gabler's Economic Lexicon]*, is that it only seems plausible for closed economies. 'In open economies, the accumulation of excess savings would flow abroad, cause devaluation of the domestic currency and, via an increase in goods exports, trigger an expansionary multiplier process. A decline in domestic national income need not then occur.'[93]

The idea that the phenomenon of secular stagnation no longer applies in the event of capital export is wrong. The very fact that capital export is taking place shows that domestic savings are not being completely converted into demand and are thus being exported as capital export together with the export surpluses. Capital export is thus only a temporary guarantee that the economic demand gap can be closed. The export surplus does not constitute

---

[92]Hans-Werner Wohltmann: *Säkulare Stagnation [Secular Stagnation]* in:http://wirtschaftslexikon.gabler.de/Definition/saekulare-stagnation.html

[93] Hans-Werner Wohltmann: loc.cit..

additional demand capable of triggering a multiplier effect. A multiplier effect can only be set off by enabling additional demand abroad by creating money over and above real savings.

Ultimately, not even Keynes believed in saturation, '"as long as not everyone is driving a Rolls Royce" and drinking champagne'[94]. What was evidently not taken on board, however, was the fact that economic development is linked to a shift in the distribution of wealth and income in the direction of the few, meaning that it is not widespread saturation that causes secular stagnation but predominantly the high savings rates of those on the highest incomes, who already drive Rolls Royces and drink champagne, while lower earners and the unemployed become more and more impoverished and the state is no longer able to make important infrastructure investments.

Since private economic demand is now lagging behind market supply, we are once again seeing *secular stagnation* like that of the past. Furthermore, neoclassical economic theory does not adequately differentiate pseudo-growth from real growth in the interest of the economy as a whole.

1. Only seeming growth, once the impact on economic growth of costs for the protection of resources and the reparation of environmental damage are taken into account

Neoclassical theory implicitly equates economic growth with the improvement of general prosperity. Economic activity, however, uses up natural resources, and the quicker an economy grows, the more resources it uses. This is why there have been debates about the limits of fossil fuel reserves and other raw materials needed by industry at least ever since the publications released by the *Club of Rome*. Environmental damage is another consequence of growing industrialisation and excessive agricultural production. This damage to the environment is robbing more and more living creatures of their habitats, and also poses a risk to the living conditions of human beings.

---

[94] Gerhard Willke: John Maynard Keynes: Eine Einführung, Campus Verlag Frankfurt/M. – New York 2002, p. 45f.

In order to avert these dangers, raw materials must be recovered or replaced and environmental damage must be repaired. If and where this does prove possible, it will require an ever greater financial commitment. When these costs are properly taken into account in economic growth analyses, they raise the question of whether or not economic successes actually compensate for costs linked to the protection of our environment and our health. If they do not, this would mean our economy is in fact already stagnating.

2. False equation of economic growth with the improvement of general prosperity

It is assumed as a matter of course that economic growth leads to improvements in general prosperity. In fact, however, it is only possible to equate these two things if the income of all the members of an economy is growing to the same extent.

Historically, however, income has not tended to grow equally across all income brackets. This is confirmed by French economist Thomas Piketty in his latest book, *Capital in the Twenty-First Century*, which is expected to appear in German next year, and is already available in English.

Carsten Brönstrup writes: 'Piketty has triggered a debate about inequality and one-sided economic policy in a way no economist has done for a long time. "The most important economics book of the year, possibly the decade," raves Nobel Prize winner Paul Krugman. Even Pope Francis recently announced on Twitter that inequality is "the root of social evil". In painstaking detail, Piketty has compiled data on income, growth and prosperity from 30 countries over 200 years of economic history.'[95]

'At the core of the book is the rule "r>g". Over the long term, the rate of return - "r" - on shares, bonds or real estate amounts to between 4.5 and 5% per year according to Piketty's calculations. The usual growth rate of the economy ("g") - and thus the income from

---

[95] Carsten Brönstrup: *Der Kapitalismus nützt nur den Wohlhabenden, sagt der Ökonom Thomas Piketty. Nur mit höheren Steuern lässt sich das System retten [Capitalism Only Benefits the Wealthy, Says Economist Thomas Piketty: Only Higher Taxes Can Save the System]*, in: DER TAGESSPIEGEL NO. 22 048 / 18. 5. 2014, P. 22

work - only amounts to between 1 and 1.5% over the long term.'[96] This means, as Patrick Welter puts it: 'When the return on capital is greater than the growth rate of the real economy, capital becomes increasingly concentrated in the hands of a few families.'[97] 'Working hard in order to one day become part of the elite in society remains, therefore, a utopia - at least for those without means. Instead of prosperity for all, the system only permits wealth for the few. And the goal of policies to create a fairer society through education would thus be unachievable.'[98]

Where does this inequality come from?

Rationalisation investments cause profits to rise at employees' expense. In other words: the share taken by employers and holders of capital increases to the extent that wages fall, minus revenue losses resulting from price reductions. In this way, income distribution shifts in their favour.

When workers who are laid off as a result of rationalisation do not find new jobs generated by investments in expansion and the production of new products and services, unemployment arises. This increases the supply of labour, with the result that wages fall again and the income share of employers and capitalists increases even further.

Even more severe shifts in income distribution in the direction of the few come about as a result of the fact that the wealthy are naturally able to save more, so they earn additional income from asset investments. These assets are then passed down as inheritance, without sufficient amounts being fed back to the community in the form of inheritance tax. In this way, the accumulation of wealth in the hands of the few can continue at an ever-increasing rate.

---

[96] Carsten Brönstrup, loc. cit.
[97] Patrick Welter: *Thomas Piketty Ein Rockstar-Ökonom erobert Amerika [Thomas Piketty: A Rockstar Economist Conquers America]*, in: FAZ Wirtschaft,http://www.faz.net/aktuell/wirtschaft/menschen-wirtschaft/thomas-piketty-ein-rockstar-oekonom-erobert-amerika-12931937.html
[98] Carsten Brönstrup, loc. cit.

12552: Income distribution in the USA 1967 – 2005 (Share of the top quintile by household income)

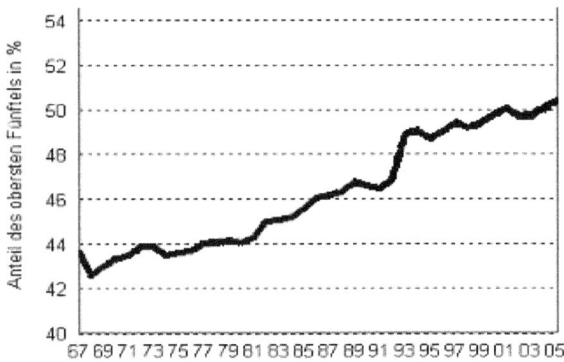

Quelle: U.S. Census Bureau. © Jahnke - Http.//www.jjahnke.net

In Germany too we have seen big changes in income distribution, as is clear from the following table:

Composition of the German population according to income bracket

	1986	1996	2006
High income earners	5.3	6.4	9.2
Top income bracket	10.9	11.6	11.3
Middle income earners	63.2	61.3	54.1
Middle income bracket			
Low income earners	8.5	7.5	7.2
Lowest income bracket	12.1	13.2	18.3
in %			

Source: SOEP (Socio-Economic Panel)/DIW (German Institute for Economic Research), (2008) (net household income weighted according to need)[99]

---

[99] cited in: Meinhard Miegel, Stefanie Wahl, Martin Schulte: *Die Einkommensentwicklung ausgewählter Bevölkerungsgruppen in Deutschland [Income Development of Selected Population Groups in Germany]*, p. 16.

The changes in the composition of the population according to income bracket can be seen in the following overview:

Changes in the composition of the population according to income bracket between 1996 and 2006
in millions

Total population	Low income earners	Middle income earners	High income earners
+0.7	+4.1	-5.5	+2.1

Source: SOEP (Socio-Economic Panel)/DIW (German Institute for Economic Research), (2008) (net household income weighted according to need) and calculations by the Bonn Institute for Economic and Social Research[100]

In 2006, in his book *Falsch globalisiert*[101] *[Wrongly Globalised]*, Joachim Jahnke has this to say on the subject: 'The USA has by far the greatest inequality in income distribution of all the highly developed industrialised nations. The contrast to Germany is stark: in the USA the difference between the shares of total income received by the top 10% of earners and the bottom 10% is almost twice as large as in Germany. The top quintile, following an inexorable ascent (...) now monopolises just over half of all income (...) It can come as no surprise, therefore, that the Federal Reserve also noted an unequal increase in wealth in "Recent Changes in U. S. Family Finances": the wealth of the top 10% of households grew by more than 90% between 1992 and 2001. The top 1% of households already owned 30% of all assets, and the top 10% as much as 65% (Figure for Germany: 47%). The trend towards increasing inequality is likely to have continued in recent years, especially given that the stock markets have now recovered. The increase in the number of millionaires, of which there were already 7.9 million in 2006, is symptomatic of this trend.'[102]

Since 2006, Germany has caught up. Andreas Oswald points out: 'The rich are getting richer, while the middle class and the

---

[100] cited in: Meinhard Miegel, loc. cit., p. 18.
[101] Joachim Jahnke: *Falsch globalisiert [Wrongly Globalised]*.
[102] http://www.jjahnke.net/us.html

poor are staying where they are. This hypothesis, posited by French economist Thomas Piketty and currently dominating the social inequality debate, has acquired a new urgency. The *New York Times* has analysed income data collected by the independent institute Luxembourg Income Study (LIS), and has come to an alarming conclusion, particularly for Americans. According to the data, the middle class in the USA no longer earns more than the middle classes of all the other large industrialised nations - an advantage it took for granted just 30 years ago. ... The lower classes in Europe now earn more than the lower class in the USA. The reason for this is that over the past 35 years in the USA, only a small stratum of rich people have profited from economic growth. ... Germany is the only country in Europe to have actually widened the gap between itself and the USA between 1980 and 2010 in terms of the income of the middle class. All other countries saw a narrowing of the income gap. This is in reference to a thirty-year period. The most dramatic development for the USA - and for Germany - was over a shorter period. Since the year 2000, the incomes of the middle class in the USA have only risen by 0.3%. In Germany they have risen by 1.4%, so only slightly more,'[103] If economic growth is taken to mean an increase in *general* prosperity, then this development is evidence to the contrary.

Supply-oriented neoclassicists even go so far as to claim that unequal income distribution is favourable to growth. If more money is saved as a result of unequal income distribution, then - so their ideology would have it - more is invested, and more investment means - again a simplification which fails to take into account rationalisation investments - more jobs. But when real economic investment opportunities do not keep pace with growing savings, a demand gap is created - and that means secular stagnation. Even the managers of limited companies will then opt to increase the profit per share by buying back treasury shares rather than through real economic investment because, according to Mar-

---

[103] Andreas Oswald: *Die Mittelschicht verliert Alarmierende neue Zahlen: In den USA und in Deutschland bleibt sie vom Wachstum ausgeschlossen [The Middle Classes Are Losing Out // Alarming New Figures: In the USA and Germany the Middle Classes Are Not Benefiting From Growth]*, in: DER TAGESSPIEGEL No.22025, 24/4/2014, p.24.

tin Wolf, 'it is easy for them to control share prices (thus securing their bonus payments) through share buybacks, meaning they do not have to go down the more difficult route of more productive investments.'[104]

Neoclassical economic theory, of course, does not see these problems. Thus the stock exchanges celebrate rises in the share price of corporations that rationalise their profit by cutting jobs and, as a result of the much-vaunted focus on core competency, shed branches of production in order to buy competitor companies which they use to rationalise their production still further, the better to monopolise the market. However, this process causes a significant shift away from wage incomes in favour of capital incomes, thereby increasing still further the supply of capital for which there are not enough real economic investments as it is.

The way in which economic activity is controlled from a stock market point of view can be seen from the evaluation of Siemens' returns in relation to other corporations, particularly General Electric. On 3 and 4 October, *Die Welt* reported on 'the expectations of the financial markets, which are anticipating a rate of return of at least 12%, a figure that Kaeser's predecessor Peter Löscher failed to achieve. The gap between Siemens and its competitors General Electric and ABB is seen as unacceptable. Analysts from J. P. Morgan think the problem lies in the fact that Siemens is taking on orders so as to ensure capacity utilisation and to safeguard jobs, but that these orders are failing to hit profit targets.'[105]

The stock exchange calculates the return on shares using a combination of dividends and share prices, as can be seen from the following 'return triangles':

---

[104] According to *K. Singer:* Summers: Secular stagnation described by Martin Wolf in the FT under the heading 'Why the future looks sluggish'. Source: http://www.timepatternanalysis.de/Blog/2013/11/21/summers-sakulare-stagnation/

[105] Elisabeth Zimmermann: Siemens verschärft Arbeitsplatzabbau [Siemens intensifies job cuts], in:
https://www.wsws.org/de/articles/2013/10/08/siem-o08.html

2004	-1.8									
2005	6.8	16.1								
2006	5.8	9.8	3.8							
2007	14.4	20.4	22.6	44.9						
2008	-3.7	-4.1	-10.1	-16.3	-51.6					
2009	0.2	0.6	-3.0	-5.1	-23.2	21.9				
2010	5.6	6.8	5.1	5.4	-5.2	32.7	44.4			
2011	1.9	2.5	0.4	-0.3	-9.2	12.0	7.3	-20.2		
2012	2.9	3.5	1.8	1.5	-5.5	11.8	8.6	-5.8	11.2	
2013	4.6	5.3	4.0	4.1	-1.5	13.5	11.5	2.3	15.9	20.8
Ø	3.7	6.7	3.1	4.9	-16.0	18.4	17.9	-7.9	13.5	20.8
	2003	2004	2005	2006	2007	2008	2009	2010	2011	2012

>>**Siemens Return Triangle**

The return triangle shows the average yearly returns for given investment periods, i.e. combinations of purchase and sale dates on a yearly basis. The horizontal access shows the year of purchase and the vertical access shows the year of sale. The average (annualised) return achieved can be read off at the intersection of the two coordinates. For example: Someone who bought Siemens shares at the end of 2003 and sold them again at the end of 2005, would have got an average annual price return of 6.8%. If the shares had been sold in 2006, this would have given a rate of return per annum of 5.8%.

The data in the bottom line shows what annual returns could be obtained by buying shares in the relevant year. Siemens investors who bought shares at the end of 2003, for example, obtained average annual returns of 3.7%.[106]

The stock exchange, with its primarily short-term return expectations, now compares expected Siemens returns with those of other corporations and particularly those of competitors such as General Electric.

---

[106] http://www.boerse.de/performance/Siemens/DE0007236101

2004	8.2									
2005	9.2	10.2								
2006	4.7	2.9	-3.9							
2007	0.7	-1.7	-7.2	-10.4						
2008	-14.4	-19.3	-27.2	-36.7	-55.2					
2009	-13.1	-16.9	-22.5	-27.9	-35.3	-6.7				
2010	-8.0	-10.5	-14.2	-16.5	-18.5	10.0	29.6			
2011	-7.0	-8.9	-11.8	-13.3	-14.0	6.9	14.4	1.0		
2012	-5.0	-6.6	-8.8	-9.5	-9.4	8.1	13.5	6.3	11.8	
2013	-2.0	-3.0	-4.6	-4.7	-3.7	12.2	17.5	13.8	20.7	30.4
Ø	-2.7	-6.0	-12.5	-17.0	-22.7	6.1	18.8	7.0	16.3	30.4
	2003	2004	2005	2006	2007	2008	2009	2010	2011	2012

'General Electric Return Triangle'[107]

This shows that if a General Electric share is bought in 2012 and sold in 2013, a return of 30.4% is achieved, while a Siemens share only gives a return of 20.8%. This gives rise to the demand that, in order to meet the criteria of the capital market, Siemens must rationalise, cut jobs and focus on core competences. The fact that a Siemens share was bought in 2003 and sold in 2013 generated an average return of 3.7%, whereas a General Electric share bought and sold at the same times generated an average loss of 2.7%, is not taken into account.

Partly to comply with stock market expectations, Siemens cuts jobs. Die Wirtschaftswoche writes: 'One thing is certain - employees' worries are not over yet. Because in addition to the 15,000 jobs cuts announced by Siemens last Autumn, there are now plans to axe even more, as Kaeser stated today. Several thousand jobs could go.'[108] In order to reinforce its core competency, Siemens is also selling businesses to competitors and buying businesses from competitors.

In what way are these rationalisations and reinforcements of core competency supposed to increase general prosperity?

---

[107] http://www.boerse.de/performance/General-Electric/US3696041033
[108] http://www.wiwo.de/unternehmen/industrie/siemens-konzernumbau-die-neue-siemens-welt/9857238-2.html

Cutting jobs in order to increase profits shifts economic income from employees to capitalists, and into higher bonuses for executives. If the higher profits and the resulting additional savings can be invested back into the real economy to a sufficient extent, then workers who have been laid off will be able to find new jobs. In a period of secular stagnation, however, this does not happen. Economic demand also declines, therefore, to the extent that workers are laid off, unless it can be reinstated through higher credit-financed state spending, or through capital export or capital burning on the capital market.

Where rationalisation increases competition and leads to reductions in price, the purchasing power of the remaining consumers may grow. The drop in profits resulting from price reductions is then supposed to be offset by a higher market share, reducing competing companies' ability to produce and to employ people. This also leads to an increase in the monopolisation of supply, meaning profits rise again at the expense of consumers.

The reinforcement of core competencies is another way in which competition is restricted. Some argue that concentrating on a few products facilitates development potential. But is it not much more likely to be the case that increased competition leads to increased research and development while monopolisation reduces the pressure to carry out research and development?

Fundamental research is too expensive for most businesses. That is why ground-breaking innovation is often the result of fundamental research - and particularly military research - financed by public money. Look at the invention of radar, the Internet etc.![109]

Rationalising companies do not care where additional profits come from. The capital market simply expects, as in Siemens' case, that a 12% profit rate will be achieved. But why do shareholders actually need to get a 12% return if their needs are already met, and when in periods of secular stagnation savers are only getting a little over 0% in interest on their savings? Apart from the fact that

---

[109] For example, in Germany research that helps to promote economic development is carried out by the 'Max Planck Institutes' (formerly the 'Kaiser Wilhelm Institutes'). See Petersen: Wirtschaftsethik und Wirtschaftspolitik [Economic Ethics and Economic Policy], p.165ff.

the market itself no longer fulfils supply-oriented expectations in times of secular stagnation, the central problem is still the income gap between high and low earners.

This seems to be gradually filtering through even to liberal economic policymakers. Andreas Oswald writes: 'Piketty's empirical findings [in his new book *Capital in the Twentieth-First Century*] that returns for owners of capital are rising faster than the growth of economies and the incomes of the wider population, are grist to the mill for everyone who has long been calling for heavier taxation of wealth.

One very important point made by Thomas Piketty has now been backed up by the International Monetary Fund (IMF). According to a new IMF study cited by the Financial Times on Wednesday, greater equality does not have a negative impact on growth. More equality could even encourage growth. This certainly puts a damper on the hypothesis which has prevailed up to now, that inequality and disparity are drivers of growth.'[110]

3. The problematic equation of economic growth with improvements in general prosperity over the course of globalisation

The original source of economic prosperity is having the greatest possible division of labour. Each individual specialises in what he or she does best, increasing the productivity of the economy for everybody. The greatest possible division of labour goes beyond national borders; the Scottish moral philosopher and national economist Adam Smith, in his 1776 book *The Wealth of Nations*, advocated free trade as the source of general economic prosperity.

---

[110] Andreas Oswald: *Die Mittelschicht verliert Alarmierende neue Zahlen: In den USA und in Deutschland bleibt sie vom Wachstum ausgeschlossen [The Middle Classes Are Losing Out // Alarming New Figures: In the USA and Germany the Middle Classes Are Not Benefiting From Growth]*, in: DER TAGESSPIEGEL No.22025, 24/4/2014, p.24.

Free trade also makes it possible to exploit regional differences in the distribution of mineral resources and skills. Free trade was thus the source of globalisation. Free trade and globalisation became central tenets of liberal and neoclassical economic theory.

But too little consideration was given to technological progress and the concentration of private power in the hands of global businesses and oligarchs, in terms of the effect this would have on general economic prosperity.

3.1 Insufficient attention to the detrimental impact on general prosperity of the distribution of technical and economic know-how in the course of globalisation

If international free trade is only about the exchange of products which logically can only be produced in individual countries - pepper in Asia, for example, or cocoa and coffee in tropical countries, which are then exchanged for amber from the Baltic Sea - or the trade of artefacts which are traditionally made differently in individual countries, then no restructuring is needed in the individual countries themselves. Each country simply produces more, and exchanges the goods produced for other goods from other countries. When technological progress and industrial production come into play, this is no longer the case. Products can then be manufactured more cheaply using industrialised processes, making craftsmen in other countries unemployed. This process began with English cloth production, which spread throughout Europe plunging artisanal weavers into poverty, and which still costs independent textile producers in developing countries their livelihoods to this day, unless they are prepared to work on a contract basis for international textile firms.

Aside from the fact that international competition for such contract manufacturing often enables companies to pay less than a living wage, independent artisanal textile producers in other countries are robbed of their livelihoods. Just look at all the products, including used textiles, soft toys, plastic toys etc., that are, it is fair to say, *dumped* on the markets of developing countries, destroying their domestic manufacturing.

In agricultural production too, yields were increased to such an extent (in the industrialised nations in particular) that developing countries using traditional methods fell behind, with the result that in certain countries it is no longer worth farming cereals, cattle or poultry, for example.

Less developed countries are also at a disadvantage compared to developed countries in that the demand for industrial goods in general is higher than that for traditionally manufactured products. For this reason, trade has developed best between industrialised nations. The less industry a country has, the smaller its importance in international trade, unless the developing country possesses energy reserves or other sought-after raw materials. But in that case only a few low-skilled workers are required - or, if the raw material extraction process is very capital-intensive, even fewer highly skilled workers. Usually only a small upper class benefits from the profits, while the rest of the country sinks into poverty and backwardness. It is only in countries where the profit from raw materials is as high as it is in the Gulf states, and it is spread across a relatively small domestic population, that the domestic population participates in the profits and exploitation and poverty are limited to migrant workers - who still earn more than they would in their home countries, however.

Proportionately, moreover, developed countries always earn more from international trade than developing countries. More money can be made from diversified industrial products than from agricultural production and raw materials. Furthermore, the industrialised nations control transport and trade routes and to the extent that human labour is replaced by real capital, the return on that capital also flows to them.

'Over the past two decades, globalisation has primarily increased prosperity in the industrialised nations. Emerging and developing countries, on the other hand, have benefited comparatively little. This is one of the key results of a study by the Bertelsmann Foundation on the effects of globalisation in 42 countries. According to the study, the fact that the world has got smaller has done nothing to shrink the wealth gap between industrialised countries like Finland, Denmark and Japan and the emerging countries - quite the reverse, in fact. While the effects of globalisation caused gross domestic product per capita in the top 20 industrialised nations to rise by an average of around 1000 Euros a year, in countries like Mexico, China and India it rose by less than 100 Euros per person.[111]

With regard to the relationship between global economic demand and global economic supply, it is also important to take into account the fact that the needs of industrialised countries are usually met more fully, meaning that more is saved in industrialised countries and that global economic consumer demand decreases accordingly. For classical market theorists, however, this problem does not exist. They work on the assumption that there are always enough profitable investment opportunities available and that all savings reappear on the real economic market as investment demand.

The market can only be a source of general prosperity if the unequal industrial and asset-centred structures which destroy market equilibrium can be counteracted. The only countries that were able to halt the one-sided development from which only the industrialised nations were benefiting were the countries that restricted imports from companies who said they were not prepared to relocate some of their production to the country itself. In this way, manufacturing know-how and skilled workforces were generated in emerging countries. This policy only works, though, in countries which represent a big enough market for a foreign investor.

With the increasing improvements to production conditions in emerging countries, however, the traditional industrialised nations themselves began to experience increasing levels of *deindustrialisation*. If companies could and had to produce in emerging countries, it was only worth their while to do so in suitably large volumes, taking advantage of cheap wage costs in the process.

---

[111] Study by Prognos AG, commissioned by the Bertelsmann Foundation:*Industrienationen profitieren von der Globalisierung weitaus stärker als Schwellen- und Entwicklungsländer [Industrialised Nations are Benefiting from Globalisation Much More than Emerging and Developing Countries]*, Pressemeldung Gütersloh, 24/03/2014, http://www.bertelsmann-stiftung.de/cps/rde/xchg/bst/ hs.xsl/nachrichten_120603.htm

The neoliberals did not see deindustrialisation as a problem. Instead it was celebrated as societal progress, one step closer to a *service economy*. Liberals see the transition to a service economy as progress because they believe it causes lower skilled jobs to be replaced by higher quality and (as was initially thought) more secure ones.

This did not entirely prove to be the case, however. In practice, service jobs turned out to be at least as insecure as industrial ones, due to digitalisation and computerisation in the name of rationalisation, and due to foreign outsourcing - we need only look at telephone helplines for evidence of this. The transition to a service economy did enable the economies in question to achieve growth, particularly when it came to the expansion of financial services. However, this growth was predominantly felt in the profits of capital holders and the salaries of highly qualified employees.

In the course of rationalisation investments, moreover, wages again turned into profits. One need only think of the vast profits made by internet companies at the expense of traditional commercial channels. Lower income earners participated very little, if at all, in this growth, and many fell even further into the precariat, which has to be subsidised by the state.

Ulrich Herbert has this to say of Andreas Wirsching's book *Das neue Europa entsteht im Geist des Neoliberalismus [The New Europe is Being Built in a Spirit of Neoliberalism]*: 'One of the most interesting aspects of this book are the sections about Europe and globalisation. The European Union emerges as one of the biggest propagandists of neoliberalism. In the 1990s, the continental industrialised nations were still lagging behind when it came to the Anglo-Saxon model of the flexibilised service economy. The 'Lisbon Strategy' of March 2000 focused on making the Union into 'the most competitive and most dynamic knowledge-based economic area in the world'. Globalisation, pluralisation, knowledge economy, flexibilisation, benchmarking: terms like this began to catch on, and soon dominated political target-setting. European Union documents increasingly began to use the language of management consultants - a kind of new modernisation ideology which, in practice, quickly started to reveal its downsides. Wirsching writes: 'By liberalising, deregulating and privatising, governments gave a lasting boost to the power of the market, and granted more elbowroom to big corporations and banks. In doing so, of course, they themselves paved the way for the very loss of sovereignty which they complained so bitterly about later on.' The result was the flexible service economy in which the old working class was replaced by the precariat with its 'bad jobs', which do not pay enough to live on and which therefore have to be subsidised by the state.'[112]

Where the transition to a service economy causes income distribution to shift further in the direction of the rich with their high savings rates, secular stagnation is exacerbated still further. And quite apart from this fact, the impoverishment of low income earners and an increase in the number of people who are unemployed can hardly be classed as an improvement in general prosperity.

While developing countries must try, as globalisation marches on, to ensure that they participate sufficiently in technological progress and that they also impose import restrictions in defiance of the market ideologues, the industrialised nations must make sure that the lower skilled workers in their countries are able to find jobs and are adequately paid, and that wages do not sink to the level of those in developing countries.

When individual countries have specific raw materials, tourist attractions and agricultural production possibilities at their disposal, specialising in particular economic activities in the area of international trade is sensible and even necessary. But when production and industrial services are founded solely on technical and economic know-how, they can potentially happen anywhere. This is why technical and economic know-how should not be used to concentrate production and services but to facilitate the most diverse activity possible, everywhere. After all, there is no country in the world which is home solely to highly qualified academics or to unskilled workers, nor does it contribute to general prosperity to have engineers and skilled workers forced to emigrate to Germany, for example, and unskilled German workers reduced to earning wages equivalent to those in developing countries. This, however,

---

[112] Ulrich Herbert on Andreas Wirsching *Das neue Europa entsteht im Geist des Neoliberalismus [The New Europe is Being Built in a Spirit of Neoliberalism]* in: Süddeutsche Zeitung, 13/03/2012, S.2.
http://herbert.geschichte.uni- freiburg.de/ herbert/beitraege/2012/ Wirsching-%20Preis%20der%20Freiheit-%20SZ%2012.3.2012.pdf

is where an unchecked development of the market economy as advocated by the neoclassicists would lead. Aspirations such as the introduction of a minimum wage, rules on the posting of construction workers, trade restrictions and subsidies to promote diversified economic development are all thorns in the side of the neoclassicists. They conveniently forget their lofty goals of letting the economy be ruled entirely by the market, however, when the interests of big corporations are at stake: when mass production by large-scale agricultural operations destroys agriculture in developing countries, for example.

Agriculture in developing countries can also be destroyed by investors buying up huge tracts of land for mass production, of bio-energy or animal feed, for example, thereby rendering traditional farmers unemployed. These farmers then make up a percentage of the refugees who migrate to industrialised nations in search of work.

Luke Dale Harris writes of the developments in Romania: 'Amid the hysteria surrounding Romanian immigration at the beginning of this year [2014], something crucial was forgotten: borders in the EU often open both ways. While newspapers in Western Europe bemoaned the impending "onslaught" of migrant workers, there was a very different invasion in the making. It was linked to the fact that, for new EU Member States like Romania, the honeymoon period had now come to an end. From 2014, the country was obliged to open up its own land market to foreign investors.

For a country with almost 5 million peasant farmers - a quarter of the population - this was no cause for celebration. The farming economy, predominantly made up of smallholders, has long been eroding under the open-market policies from which it derives zero benefit. Squeezed out of the market by the agri-investment giants who pocket most of the EU's common agricultural policy subsidies, Romanian small farmers face a difficult choice: sell up and move to Western Europe to look for work, or hold tight and sink even further into poverty. ... The communal, state-owned lands on which, until 1990, 90% of farmers still grazed their livestock, have completely disappeared. They have been leased to foreign companies, or sold off.'[113]

Of course, the buying up of land increases productivity. But the profits flow straight back to those whose standard of living is already assured - all they will do with these profits is use them for speculation, while secular stagnation ensures that hardly any new jobs will be created for the workers who have lost theirs.

3.2 Insufficient attention to the detrimental impact on general prosperity of the narrow concentration of private economic power and its unequal distribution in the course of globalisation

The central objective of liberal neoclassical economic theory is the greatest possible degree of free self-determination by individuals, not only as an end in itself but also as a prerequisite for a functioning market, which in turn is seen as the best possible way to ensure economic growth and a general improvement in living standards. According to the liberal economic view, pure self-interest is enough to motivate economic operators - in compliance with market rules, of course - to work towards this goal, since personal profit will be higher the more the goods and services are demanded by market participants. The market economy is thus equated with fair competition, as a result of which everybody is rewarded according to the services they provide.

Fair competition, however, calls for equality of opportunity. Boxers only fight other boxers of the same weight category, for instance; men compete against men, women against women, disabled athletes against other disabled athletes. Equal starts like this do not exist in the free market economy. The starting conditions of market participants are significantly affected by the wealth they own. This is partly because, on top of earned income (from a job),

---

[113] Luke Dale Harris: *Bauernlegen auf Europäisch Rumänien Die traditionelle Landwirtschaft hat ausgedient. Sie wird durch ein ausuferndes Land Grabbing überrollt [Clearing Peasants the European Way // Romania // The end is nigh for traditional farming. It is being engulfed by land grabbing on a huge scale]* in: der Freitag, No. 19, 8 May 2014, p. 8.

a market participant who owns wealth can make money by exploiting that wealth. It is also due to the fact that wealth can be used as security to obtain credit.

If market participants have acquired their wealth themselves, it may still be compatible with fair competition for this same wealth to be invested for a profit. But what about inherited wealth? Some people inherit so much wealth that they do not even need to work anymore, and can live off the returns on their assets. In such a situation we can hardly speak of equality of opportunity for everybody.

Economic development also requires investment, and investment requires savings. Because unequal income distribution encourages saving, it also encourages economic development, though only for as long as there are enough real economic investment opportunities to invest savings in. When savings overtake investment opportunities, as we have seen, secular stagnation arises.

As regards the ideal of freedom and individual citizens' opportunities for personal development - which are also an element of general well-being, after all - the 'uncontrolled market economy' pattern of wealth development actually undermines its own goals and does not use the creative potential of all citizens in the best possible way. This also applies to the relationships between individual countries.

In closed economies, national market conditions, taxes and spending can be coordinated using the necessary state regulations. In a global economy, international trade involves more than just the exchange of goods that one country is better able to produce than another: it also gives rise to companies which operate internationally and have branches and production facilities in several different countries.

These global companies are managed from their home states. And the most highly skilled jobs are located in these home states. This usually makes it difficult for developing countries to offer employment opportunities to more highly skilled employees and entrepreneurs. Correspondingly, most of the taxes these companies generate are paid in their home states, because that is where the profits and the higher wages and salaries are. But it is more lucrative still for a country not only to act as a base for international companies but also to develop into a financial centre; because a lot more money can be made through capital market transactions than in the real economy.

Companies that operate internationally can, however, also evade national restrictions and regulations which do not work in their favour by relocating production capacity and logistical centres, To avoid paying tax, transactions can be carried out via letterbox companies in tax havens. Companies also reap the benefits of certain states offering special incentives and tax advantages if a company transfers its head office, profit centre or production operations to their country.

Because capitalists operate so independently of their countries of residence and are able to manage their companies worldwide in their own interests, states become increasingly powerless to stop this development and to combat the resulting crises.

This competition between nations for businesses and rich citizens has forced states to lower their taxes ever further in the attempt to prevent an exodus. So additional state spending has been financed by public borrowing rather than by raising taxes, and where public debt reaches its limits, social spending and vital public investment is cut rather than increase the tax burden on businesses and the rich.

When states raise taxes, as in France for example, capitalists and businesses threaten to emigrate. Neoclassicists also like to argue that lower corporate taxes stimulate the economy. After the last war, taxes in the USA were close to 90%, and in Germany 30 years ago the top rate of income and corporation tax still stood at 56% plus trade tax, without the economy having suffered as a result of the high rate of income tax up to that point.

Nations' dependence upon international companies is assuming ever more dramatic proportions. A single management board resolution is enough to close down production facilities in one country and relocate them to another. Through corporate lobbying, companies are able to influence legislation planning, setting standards that extend even to seed modifications and potato varieties which they themselves earn money from through license payments.

Via the liberalised capital market, speculative money and capital can be very quickly pumped into particular regions, and withdrawn again. Such transactions can occur without the country in question having done anything to prompt them. They may be triggered by nothing more than investment pressure causing capitalists to transfer capital to riskier regions, only to withdraw it again immediately when it becomes clear that interest rates in the USA, for example, are on the rise. A sensible or a misguided remark by the head of a central bank can trigger enormous capital transactions capable of plunging countries into financial emergencies.

These problems are barely even acknowledged by neoclassicists. Instead they advocate further tariff elimination and further liberalisation of international trade and the capital market. This is demonstrated very clearly in their support for the planned Transatlantic Trade and Investment Partnership (TTIP). Wikipedia states: 'According to official statements, the treaty will stimulate economic growth in the participating countries, cut unemployment and increase workers' average incomes, among other things. Leading representatives from the European Union, like José Manuel Barroso, US president Obama, the German chancellor Angela Merkel and many other leading politicians, have repeatedly emphasised the necessity and the positive effects of the treaty. Merkel said in February 2013: "We would like nothing better than to see a free trade agreement between Europe and the United States".[114][115][116][117] <<[118]

---

[114] German Foreign Office, 19 June 2013: *Präsident Obama in Berlin – Noch enger zusammenrücken mit einer Freihandelszone [President Obama in Berlin – Moving Even Closer Together With A Free Trade Area]*

[115] *USA und EU forcieren gigantische Freihandelszone [USA and EU Push For Huge Free Trade Area]*, Die Welt, Chancellor Angela Merkel: "We would like nothing better than to see a free trade agreement between Europe and the United States", in Berlin on 3 February 2013 to the Federal Association of German Industry, and "Sooner or later even the most difficult projects come to fruition", also in Berlin on 4 February 2013, at a reception for the diplomatic corps.

[116] Thorsten Jungholt, Clemens Wergin: *Sicherheitskonferenz: USA und EU forcieren gigantische Freihandelszone [Security Conference:USA and EU Push For Huge Free Trade Area]*, Die Welt 2. February 2013

[117] *Statement by José Manuel BARROSO, President of the EC, on the TTIP*:You Tube

[118] http://de.wikipedia.org/wiki/Transatlantisches_Freihandelsabkommen

What is leading the politicians to make such optimistic forecasts? The Bertelsmann study *The Transatlantic Trade and Investment Partnership (TTIP), Who benefits from a transatlantic trade treaty?* is typical of neoclassical calculations of increased prosperity through liberalisation. *Part 1: Macroeconomic Effects.*

The study foresees only minor benefits in a further reduction of tariffs, since the tariffs between America and Europe are already very low anyway. But it claims that prosperity would be significantly increased if non-tariff barriers were also lifted. In particular, the study forecasts that:

'1. Trade between the USA and Germany will be only marginally increased by the abolition of customs duties. Lifting non-tariff barriers as well, as part of a comprehensive liberalisation scenario, will have a much greater impact. The predicted benefits are in the region of 90%. ...

4. Germany's trade with the BRICS states (Brazil, Russia, India, China, South Africa) would be reduced by around 10%, relative to the final balance of trade, as a result of the comprehensive agreement. Compared to the huge expansion in transatlantic trade, this is a minor effect. The USA's trade with the BRICS countries, however, would fall much more sharply (30%).

5. EU trade with neighbouring states in North Africa or Eastern Europe would be reduced by an average of 5% as a result of the comprehensive agreement. This is because the TTIP would devalue some of the existing preferential agreements...

7. The lifting of non-tariff barriers has a much larger impact on real income per capita in Europe than simply minimising customs duties. It would appear that Britain stands to benefit most from the initiative (growth of 9.70%). The Scandinavian Member States, the Baltic countries and Spain will see above-average growth. Germany, at 4.68%, will benefit a little less than the average, which stands at 4.95%.

13. ... On average in OECD countries a total of 2 million additional jobs will be created. In the customs duty scenario, the growth in employment still equates to an extra half a million jobs.[119]

How does the Bertelsmann study come to make such erroneous claims? Like all neoclassical statements, it works on the assumption that all cost savings not only represent increases in growth but also provide the means for further investment, thus generating even more growth. The issue of whether there is enough innovation for the savings resulting from cost reductions and economisation following the abolition of tariff barriers, or whether there is enough demand (backed by purchasing power) for this growth, is not even questioned. It is taken as read. There is no analysis of who profits from the cost savings and the lifting of non-tariff import restrictions, and what the savings rates of these profiteers are. There is no inquiry into whether and to what extent reducing customs duties and lifting non-tariff restrictions in customs and in governance will cause workers to be laid off by businesses, or whether these workers will be able to find new jobs. Nor do the calculations take account of any customs and excise revenue shortfalls countries may experience, and how this revenue will be replaced. It is enough to calculate cost savings and use them as a basis for predicting supply-oriented growth!

There is no questioning, either, of the effects this Transatlantic Trade and Investment Partnership will have on individual regions, and to what extent global players will become even more capable of undermining governments' legislative powers. It is a blessing that it was discovered in time that the agreement also proposes to grant global companies additional powers to sue governments for

---

[119] Gabriel Felbermayr, Benedikt Heid, Sybille Lehwald: *Die Transatlantische Handels- und Investitionspartnerschaft (THIP), Wem nutzt ein transatlantisches Freihandelsabkommen? [The Transatlantic Trade and Investment Partnership (TTIP), Who benefits from a transatlantic trade treaty?] Part 1: Macroeconomic Effects.*
http://www.bertelsmann-stiftung.de/cps/rde/xbcr/SID-291D5EE2-DADC6157/bst/xcms_bst_dms_38052_38053_2.pdf

doing anything which might have a negative impact on their profits. A sorry kind of study, but one typical of supply-oriented neoclassical economic theories and economic policy!

Scepticism about the future outcomes forecast by the study is confirmed by past experiences with other trade deals. As Jorge G. Castañeda writes: 'NAFTA brought neither the huge gains its proponents promised nor the dramatic losses its adversaries warned of. Everything else is debatable. Mexico, in particular, is a very different place today -- a multi-party democracy with a broad middle class and a competitive export economy -- and its people are far better off than ever before, but finding the source of the vast changes that have swept the country is a challenging task. It would be overly simplistic to credit NAFTA for Mexico's many transformations, just as it would be to blame NAFTA for Mexico's many failings.

The truth lies somewhere in between. Viewed exclusively as a trade deal, NAFTA has been an undeniable success story for Mexico, ushering in a dramatic surge in exports. But if the purpose of the agreement was to spur economic growth, create jobs, boost productivity, lift wages, and discourage emigration, then the results have been less clear-cut.<<[120]

'"With every trade agreement there are winners and losers", says Joy Olsen from the Washington Office on Latin America (WOLA). "NAFTA is no exception." Small and medium-sized agricultural producers in Mexico are suffering as a result of the competitive pressure from US agribusinesses. Today, Mexico is a net importer of agricultural products, Large corporations, on the other hand, have been able to profit from the free movement of goods.'[121]

---

[120] Jorge G. Castañeda: *NAFTA's Mixed Record, The View From Mexico*, published by the Council of Foreign Affairs, From our January/February 2014 Issue, http://www.foreignaffairs.com/articles/140351/jorge-g-castaneda/naftas-mixed-record

[121] Die großen Verlierer der Freihandelszone Nafta [The Big Losers in the NAFTA Free Trade Zone] in DIE WELT 23.12.2013, http://www.welt.de/wirtschaft/article123252705/Die-grossen-Verlierer-der-Freihandelszone-Nafta.html

Whilst I do point to problems with globalisation, this should not be taken as a plea for national economies. There is no doubt that we must think and act on a large scale where economics is concerned. But organisational structures must be appropriate for the economic areas in which they are implemented, and must take specific regional circumstances into account. Due to its failure to take account of specific regional features, the EU itself is already criticised for its desire to standardise everything, even down to the measurements of cucumbers. All Europeans, however, should reap the benefits of being able to live and work within a large single market.

This also means that all the countries within a community should feel a responsibility towards the others. For achieving shared prosperity for such a large economic area is a mammoth task; this is evident within the European Union, particularly in the contrast between the northern and southern countries and the eastern and western ones. It is also important to ensure that the peripheral countries are able to develop sufficiently.

It is only possible to do this by having a common foreign economic policy in relation to countries outside of Europe. Because if economic development is left up to global players and capital market funds, we will not see a balanced system of employment in which lower skilled workers as well as more highly skilled ones are paid a decent wage. Instead, competition from low-wage countries will give rise to increasingly precarious working conditions in the Community.

The less developed countries in Europe would be the worst affected. After all, the most important consideration for today's investors is the market, and what investor is going to expand production in Greece or Portugal or Romania, for example, when he or she stands to conquer a huge market in China, Brazil or Russia. Without a European foreign economic policy that promotes harmony, we will see hardly any development of wage-intensive manufacturing in the peripheral European states. Without a sensible foreign trade policy, the social tensions in Europe will reach intolerable levels, inciting xenophobia and right-wing populism.

Of course, a European foreign trade policy - and the same would naturally have to apply to other economic areas too - might not allow global companies to make full use of all their opportunities to rationalise. But, as has been shown, rationalisation mainly gives rise to higher profits for holders of capital, while jobs tend to be cut. The prices of goods might not fall quite as much. But it is better that people who are earning should pay a little more for what they consume, if that means jobs for people on lower incomes. Our main priority must no longer be capital holders' profits and compliance with the shareholder value principle - instead, we must concern ourselves with better provision and smaller disparities within society.

C. The need for a new understanding of the principles of a healthy economy and economic policy measures to combat secular stagnation and stabilise the economy

According to classical economic theory, the market should ensure that self-interest also serves to further the common good. But one of the prerequisites of a functioning market is fair competition between all citizens - and there can only be fair competition when all citizens have the same market opportunities. As a result of the extreme and ever-increasing inequality in income distribution, the market economy itself is being destroyed. *The perversion of the market economy through adherence to a feudalistic concept of income* must therefore be overcome.

Since human beings spend the greater part of their lives working within the economic system, the economy should also be the place where they find the greatest possible satisfaction and self-fulfilment in their work.

The latter plays hardly any role in neoclassical economic ideology, unless a person is using his or her particular skills in such a way that they are also earning the maximum profit. For market economists, making a profit is the true purpose of life. As long as it is qualified by the phrase 'so as to consume as much as possible', this idea may be compatible with a functioning economy - although fulfilling work, once the basic needs of life are met, can in fact give the greatest satisfaction. Only somebody for whom work is a miserable daily grind dreams of being able to consume as much as possible.

But unfortunately life is so 'unfair' that those with the greatest job satisfaction often earn much more money than the people who do not particularly enjoy their work. In the capitalist market economy, however, consumption is only a side consideration, because if all income was spent on consumption, there would be no investment and no technical and economic progress. For true market economists, therefore, profit is an end in itself; whether I need it for consumption purposes or not, I should want to maximise it, and in order to maximise it I have to reinvest any savings I make in order to earn even more.

The more capital-intensive and rationalised my production, the higher my profit. And it is taken for granted that there will always be enough investment opportunities available. Unfortunately, this expectation turns out to be a fallacy. As the general level of income rises, signs of saturation emerge, and this happens more quickly the more income rises disproportionately among the wealthy, and other sections of the population are unable to buy what they need due to unemployment or low income.

The economy then falls into a state of secular stagnation, which can give way to depression at any time if speculative bubbles burst or if governments stop borrowing or are unable to borrow any more because they are at risk of insolvency and so no-one will lend to them anymore, with the result that excess savings are not turned back into demand based on purchasing power.

This is the situation we find ourselves in today. Despite extremely low interest rates, there are not enough real economic investment opportunities to absorb savings capital. The central banks are helpless, and their continued injections of funds and cuts in interests rates will only encourage yet more speculation. National debt is so excessively high that governments are ordering *debt brakes* and trying to pay back debts, overlooking the fact that investors and creditors have no idea where to invest the repaid money and that the most they will be able to do with it is speculate - i.e. drive up the prices of shares, real estate, gold, raw materials etc.

The extent of the pressure for investors to invest is illustrated by Gerald Pilz in his book *Unusual Investments: 25 Alternatives to Fixed Deposits & Co*. The publisher summarises the book's content as follows: 'For a while now it has been clear that saving doesn't pay. The interest rates on savings accounts and fixed-term deposits are well below the rate of inflation. This is causing the value of real assets to shrink year on year. What are the alternatives? Shares, gold, home ownership? Or something completely different? In his book *Unusual Investments*, Gerald Pilz offers 25 alternatives to traditional saving. Always with the aim of maintaining and increasing the value of the assets. ... He covers a wide range of alternatives, including toys, such as teddy bears, spirits such as whisky, rum and cognac, collector's items such as collectible cards and watches, works of art such as porcelain, paintings and sculptures, natural objects such as fossils and meteorites, literary collectibles such as old books, comics and original documents, plots of land such as agricultural land or woodland, rights such as patents, and many more.[122]

It soon becomes clear that the investment suggestions all relate to existing assets rather than new products taken from the market: in other words, the recommended investments are all *objects of speculation*.

In this situation, the only way out is to remember that the point of economic activity is not the pointless maximisation of profit but the meeting of demand. This would mean replacing a *supply-oriented* economic policy with a *demand-oriented* one. Demand-oriented economic policy is less about supplying as much as possible and more about working out what there is demand for.

This does not mean getting rid of incentives for businesses to invest and expand production. On the contrary: returning purchasing power to unmet demand actually creates the most powerful incentives to expand business activities.

Before we can discuss the measures that need to be taken in order to combat secular stagnation, we must first reconsider the motives for economic activity itself. Since profit is seen as the primary motive for economic development, we must first of all ask ourselves whom this profit should be assigned to.

Up to now, the rule has been that employees receive wages and salaries only, and that only investors are entitled to profits. Executives are the only employees to participate in profits, via their bonuses. The justification given for this is that investors are liable for economic results. But every business is an endeavour in which all its employees are involved, so that, in fact, everybody bears the risk of failure.

---

[122] Gerald Pilz: *Ungewöhnliche Wertanlagen 25 Alternativen zu Festgeld & Co.* [*Unusual Investments: 25 Alternatives to Fixed Deposits & Co.*], UVK, Constance 2014

In businesses in early economies, and in craft businesses today, the employer and the investor of capital still was, or is, one and the same person. In this scenario there is still some justification for profit going exclusively to the employer because he or she is working alongside the employees, in person. In a global corporation, however, investors are completely indifferent to the fate of employees and the importance of a business to a particular region. Entire production sites and branches are closed down and/or relocated to other countries in the drive to maximise profit. In a globalised world, moreover, investors' profits can rise to such enormous levels - every mass redundancy can vastly increase the share price - that profits are no longer in any way commensurate with income. [123]

In an economy whose task is to facilitate the greatest possible fulfilment of demand, there must also be some sense of the commensurability of incomes with the service provided, and this evaluation must take account of what additional income would mean for the earner in question.

According to the marginal utility school of thought, the saturation point for consumer goods is measured in units of utility (or 'utils'). In other words, a consumer good is worth as much to the consumer as the extra satisfaction he gained from the last unit he consumed. Applied to the maximisation of profit, this would imply that the utility of additional income must progressively decline. The standard of living of a multi-billionaire is not improved one whit by earning another million or even another billion.

When economies are viewed through the lens of the optimal fulfilment of demand, the eye is drawn not only to the workers who are falling into the ranks of the precariat, but also to the insufficient funding of collective needs which affect everybody, such as:

---

[123] For more detail see: *Ist die Vergütung von Managern mit mehreren Millionen pro Jahr wirtschaftsethisch vertretbar? [Are Seven-Figure Annual Salaries for Managers Economically Ethical?]*, in: Uwe Petersen: *Unkonventionelle Betrachtungsweisen zur Wirtschaftskrise: Von Haien, Heuschrecken und anderem Getier. [Unconventional Views on the Economic Crisis: On Sharks, Locusts and Other Animals]*. Verlag Peter Lang 2011, p.87ff.

- inadequate and in some cases positively ramshackle transport infrastructure (road and rail),
- the need for increased spending on education and research and development,
- the need for additional support for families,
- the reparation of environmental damage,
- funding for huge investments in the transition to new energy sources,
- inadequate universal old age insurance and health insurance etc.

The following description of economic measures that could be used to combat secular stagnation will be labelled 'unrealistic' by advocates of the reigning economic ideology. They will come up with many arguments about how investors and employers will find ways to get round the measures or will emigrate to other countries, to the detriment of any country that does not implement supply-oriented economic policy.

The author is well aware of these arguments. They are only valid, however, insofar as given circumstances are extrapolated. Anyone who judges the future based solely on past experiences, which they have turned into principles, would not have been able to predict, years ago, that human rights abuses would be committed by heads of government, that the reunification of Germany would be brought about peacefully, that corruption with a view to securing foreign orders would now be prosecuted, that tax havens would undertake to cooperate with foreign tax authorities etc.

So too, the maximisation of profit only became a guiding principle with the advent of capitalism; before that there were other demand-oriented guiding principles, and we can - and must - return to such principles. The universal maximisation of profit is destroying society, and traditional economic policy measures to stimulate the economy are no longer working. The perversion of the market as an arena of fair competition as a result of our adherence to the feudalistic concept of property must also be overcome. These processes are difficult, of course, but vitally necessary.

I. Improving market opportunities for all citizens by overcoming the entrenched practice of feudal inheritance which is incompatible with the system

In ancient times, when hunters and gatherers had more of a sense of being members of a tribe and family, there was only a limited amount of personal property. Land and soil in particular, but also homes and tools, belonged to everybody or to the tribe or family.

Back then, areas of communal arable and pasture land were allocated to individual families to manage but passed back into common ownership after the harvest. With the progressive individualisation of human beings, the notion of property became more established and areas of land were granted as fiefs. A fief ultimately belonged to its lord, who represented the state as a whole and the vassal lost the land upon his death.

With the advent of feudalism, property - consisting of the land and everything on it, including homes and tools and ultimately even the peasants who tilled the soil - passed into the hands of the ruling families and was then passed down to their descendants as inheritance. Subjects were only able to break free of the rule of the nobility through careers at court, in the military or in the church, or by fleeing to the emerging cities.

Guildsmen, too, still thought and felt in a way that 'befitted their social status'. People only aspired to the level of income and wealth that befitted their station in life. Ruinous competition was frowned upon. In any case, the guilds only admitted as many people as were needed to provide society with the respective goods they produced.

These barriers were broken down by the Industrial Revolution and capitalism. A citizen's reputation was no longer determined by his social status but by his achievements, which were measured by how much he earned and how much wealth he acquired. The market was seen as a form of social glue and regulation which would ensure that the self-interested maximisation of profit would also further the common good.

This overlooked the fact that in order for there to be fair competition on the market, there needed to be equality of opportunity for all market participants. For this reason, individuals should only ever have been allowed to maximise their own personal profit and wealth. After death, all wealth apart from personal items should have flowed back into the general population. In relation to inheritance, however, the feudal principle was perpetuated. Where children follow in their fathers' footsteps and carry on a trade business - in other words, when they work more or less according to guild principles - the passing on of a business to a person's children might be justified. Any wealth over and above this, however, should have been fed back into society as a whole.

Trade businesses are always cited by liberals as an argument for more generous inheritance rules, but the same argument cannot be applied to large corporations. What global corporation is still personally run by descendants of the founding family? At most, the descendants of founding families may still control shareholder meetings and supervisory boards thanks to their inherited ownership - even though they are not necessarily any more qualified to do so than skilled workers without any shares. And if descendants do feel an emotional connection to the company and work to acquire the necessary skills, there is nothing to stop them working their way up to an important role within the company without owning a controlling interest. The more global the scale on which companies operate, the more anachronistic the positions of those who own inherited capital become.

In order to get rid of undesirable feudal concepts of property caused by unequal wealth development, and to prevent new ones from emerging, we must introduce adequate wealth and inheritance taxes and, if necessary, capital levies. These should of course be structured in such a way that they do not impede economically sound activities[124], but strengthen them where possible. Heirs should not have to pay so much that they must significantly curtail their standard of living. But the more the maximisation of private profit is achieved at the cost of rationalisation measures that leave people jobless, and the more investors resort to playing the capital

---

[124] See also: Petersen: *Wirtschaftsethik und Wirtschaftspolitik [Economic Ethics and Economic Policy]*, p. 406ff. and Petersen: *Unkonventionelle ...III. [Unconventional ...III]*, p. 53ff.

market, the more economic development will be end up being stimulated instead by the need to fund education, research and development and family support.

A particularly important point is the abolition of so-called ground rents. Even from the point of view of capitalism and market economics is is hard to fathom why such vast incomes are earned from ground rents in sought-after locations and through land speculation. Revenue from land should be taxed at least as highly as other income.

Given that ground rents - a relic of feudalism - are particularly incompatible with the principle that land, like water and air, belongs to everybody, plots of land should preferably only be passed down as emphyteusis with ground rents which can be adjusted in accordance with the revenue generated by the land. Existing privately-owned properties should fall back into public ownership after a period of 50 years, for example, and from then on only be given out as leasehold properties.

A better distribution of wealth, or the returning of wealth to common ownership and the use of the revenue to fund training, research and development and targeted business development, would not only improve the starting conditions of the less well-off: it would also benefit the real economy. The majority of important innovations are made not by large companies but as the result of large-scale government funding for basic key research and development.

As is shown by the example of *Silicon Valley*, technical and economic development requires as many creative people as possible, but when wealth is concentrated in very few hands, such people only have the chance to develop their skills if they have sufficient resources of their own to get started and are then able find patrons who again exploit the results to maximise their own profits.

II. The need to implement economic policy to align economic savings with real economic investment opportunities in order to overcome secular stagnation

Where collective needs must be additionally financed, all earners should contribute according to their ability to do so. The first way to do this, of course, would be to have higher taxes for higher earners and on inheritance and wealth.

Thomas Piketty also recognises the necessity of this in his new book, *Capital in the Twenty-First Century*. Carsten Brönstrup writes: 'In the 1970s, the top rate of tax in the USA still stood at over 70%. Piketty wants to see a return to these times - he wants to repair the damage of capitalism through redistribution, using a progressive wealth tax which would see millionaires hand over 2% of their property per year, and billionaires 10%. He also calls for an income tax of up to 80% for the highest earners.'[125]

Paul Krugman, as we know, wants to raise income tax as high as 91%, the level it was at just after the Second World War. He sees this as the only route to growth.

It goes without saying that supply-side economic theory rejects higher taxes. It is often objected that high inheritance taxes on assets which are invested in companies put those companies at risk. On family businesses in Germany, therefore, there is already provision for charging low inheritance tax when businesses continue to be personally run by heirs.

When we consider how high corporate taxes and taxes on high incomes were at the end of the last war, without it having stopped people from investing, any qualms people might have about higher taxes do not really follow. In order to implement this system, of course, more uniform tax rates will need to be agreed internationally, and tax avoidance will need to be prevented more effectively. I discuss my arguments and suggestions with regard to tax and toll

---

[125] Carsten Brönstrup: *Der Kapitalismus nützt nur denWohlhabenden, sagt der Ökonom Thomas Piketty. Nur mit höheren Steuern lässt sich das System retten [Capitalism Only Benefits the Wealthy, Says Economist Thomas Piketty: Only Higher Taxes Can Save the System]*, in: DER TAGESSPIEGEL NO. 22 048 / 18. 5. 2014, p. 22

problems in detail in: *Erhöhung der Staatseinnahmen zur Sanierung der Staatsfinanzen [Increasing Public Revenue to Rehabilitate Public Finances]*[126]

But apart from through tax increases, all citizens - on a means-tested basis, if this is practicable - should also be directly responsible for paying the necessary contributions for specific services, as already happens with road tax and tolls and the financing of public service broadcasters. In this way all earners, whether they had children or not, could be required to pay a nurseries and schools tax; after all, the education of the next generation is something which affects all citizens. I go into more detail on this topic in: *Unkonventionelle Betrachtungsweisen zur Wirtschaftskrise III. Was ist so Lösung der Krise zu tun? [Unconventional Views on the Economic Crisis III. What Should Be Done to Resolve the Crisis?]* Page 120 ff.)

It is also difficult to understand why there are problems in terms of inadequate pension insurance and health insurance, especially given that national product has not been shrinking but steadily rising. The reason for this, it is claimed, is that due to the ageing population an increasingly small number of workers are having to finance an increasingly large number of pensioners. But why are all earners not required to make pension and health insurance contributions, thereby guaranteeing a standard basic provision for everyone? Anyone who wants better provision can take out additional insurance.

The current social security system is failing to fulfil our duty of solidarity to provide universal social security. It even encourages job destruction through rationalisation investments. Because when jobs are cut due to rationalisation, employers' contributions to social security fall accordingly. This means that not only do we see a shift from income to capital gains, but that the owners of that capital are also no longer required to pay social security contributions.

The concerns and debates about poverty in old age, and a two-tier society in the event of illness, would be eliminated if all incomes were subjected to a social security tax - including higher salaries and incomes from pensions and other sources. Procedurally, social security contributions could be levied on all busi-

---

[126] Petersen: *Unconventional Views on the Economic Crisis III*, p. 50ff.

nesses' profits, and corresponding tax credits could enable capital owners to reduce their personal social security obligations accordingly.

Social security payments could increase to such an extent that the proportional burden on those who up to now have been solely responsible for them would fall. At the same time, the current employer's contributions would no longer be necessary, so wage-intensive companies would no longer have to bear a heavier financial than companies with fewer workers. A change like this could also help combat deindustrialisation in the industrialised nations.

III. The 're-naturalisation' of the money and capital markets

The money and capital markets are not natural phenomena, of course. What is meant by the phrase 're-naturalising the money and capital markets' is turning the capital market (as far as possible) from a casino back into an exchange of capital between those seeking real economic investment and those with savings to invest. In order to do this, the following steps are necessary:
1. the neutralisation of circulating government bonds in order to reduce currency speculation instead of acquisition by central banks
2. banking regulation
3. reform of monetary policy

1. The neutralisation of circulating government bonds in order to reduce currency speculation instead of acquisition by central banks

As outlined earlier, government bonds have no material value, because the funds raised by issuing them have flowed back into economic consumption as state spending. Even when public borrowing has been used to finance investment, it still has to count as government consumption, because it does not yield any financial profit which is retained in the form of write-offs and which can be used to pay off debts to investors.

Trying to pay off public debt, and cutting state spending in order to do so, would increase the pressure to invest capital even further in times of secular stagnation and, if creditors were unable to burn the repaid debts on the capital market, there would be a greater danger of deflation.

When even social spending is cut in order to repay debt, experience has shown that this can spark social unrest. In practice, therefore, there are hardly any real repayments of national debts; instead, repayments that become due are simply refinanced on a regular basis by taking on new debts for corresponding amounts. In effect, the old debts are merely prolonged.

Because politicians are aware of the problems associated with real repayment - even if their supply-oriented economic ideology blinds them to the widening of the demand gap resulting from it - they expect to see a reduction in the level of public debt simply through not taking on any *additional* debt. They are banking on the fact that, because of the economic growth they are still expecting to see, the ratio of debt to gross national product will fall automatically. With economic growth expected to rise by only 1 to 2 %, however, we will be waiting a long time for the debt burden to shrink to the point where distressed nations will once more be seen as creditworthy. What is more likely is that in future crises general public debt will again rise considerably.

Hopes of really being able to reduce public debt in this way - especially when economies in distressed nations are still shrinking, and probable future economic crises will lead to more big increases in general public debt - seem illusory anyway. For these reasons, the government bonds currently in circulation can justifiably be characterised as 'toxic' assets, whose value is based solely on investors' belief that they, or other investors, will refinance debts when they become due.

The amount of public *toxic assets* in circulation has now reached incredible proportions. On 14 March 2014, dpa reported: 'By the middle of last year, the volume of all the debt securities in circulation had reached an estimated total of 100 trillion US dollars (72 trillion Euros), according to the quarterly report published by the umbrella organisation for central banks. Before the collapse of Lehman Brothers in 2008, the mountain of debt had 'only' amounted to around 70 trillion dollars. BIS experts explained the sharp increase in debt by pointing out that following the financial crisis, governments and companies had issued bonds in large numbers. This was done primarily to finance economic stimulus programmes and cash injections to bail out banks. According to the BIS, by mid-June 2013 government debt had risen to 43 trillion dollars. This meant there was 80% more government debt worldwide than in mid-2007.[127]

The large quantities of circulating government securities represent huge potential for speculation, through which individual economies, but also the economy as a whole, can be destroyed. Initially a few individual states - those which are classed as insolvent - are affected. They are no longer able to borrow in order to take on new debts or pay back old ones. Sovereign default leads to a country no longer being seen as an attractive economic location. Capital leaves the country and the currency exchange rate plummets, with the result that goods become more expensive to import.

National economic problems spill over into other countries. The losses made on the devalued or worthless government bonds can bankrupt creditors who have used loans to buy them, as well as banks, with repercussions for the rest of the economy. In this way, an economic crisis in one country can turn into an international crisis or, in the case of a European country, a crisis for the whole of the Eurozone and thus, of course, for the global economy.

The flight of capital from one country to another can also cause economic problems in the latter. Switzerland, for instance, has long had to defend itself against the buying up of Swiss francs in order to stop the price of the franc being driven up too high, since this would threaten Switzerland's exports by rendering them too expensive. The countries that are first affected may not even have done

---

[127] dpa Basel:*100 Billionen Dollar Schulden Weltweit enormer Anstieg seit der Lehman-Pleite [100 Billion Dollar Debt // Huge Increase Worldwide Since the Lehman Crash]*, in: WWW.TAGESSPIEGEL.DE/WIRTSCHAFT, MONDAY 10 MARCH 2014 / NO. 21 982, P. 13.

anything to cause these movements of capital. Sometimes it is enough for the US Federal Reserve to raise its interest rate, or announce its intention to do so, to cause capital to be transferred out of developing countries and into the USA. The consequences are the depreciation of developing countries' currencies and the appreciation of the dollar: both potentially unwanted side effects.

The more government bonds are bought and sold on the capital market, the greater the potential for crises. For this reason, a reduction in the number of government bonds in circulation is necessary - not only because of the potential for national insolvency but also because the negative effects of capital transfers from one government debt to another or to another form of investment can cause economic problems.

All government bonds, as demonstrated, have no material value, meaning that the creditors of government debts hold securities which are essentially worthless. In other words: if all the entitlements and debts in the economy were netted, the apparent value of these assets would vanish into thin air. It would therefore be appropriate for all governments to declare their inability to pay or to offer settlements so that government debts and the claims associated with them would be eliminated or reduced. Although this is the usual consequence of private insolvency, governments themselves are keen to avoid making private creditors bear any losses in the event of obvious national bankruptcy. They are afraid that this would result in other countries also being seen as insolvent, banks collapsing and economic crises breaking out.

The larger the volume of government debts in circulation, the more justified this fear is. For this reason it is entirely justifiable not only to reduce the volume of government debt due to the danger of insolvency but also to remove government debts from the capital market as far as possible. But how can this be done?

We have already seen that repayments of government debts exacerbate the demand gap on the real economic market and thus increase the risk of deflation when these repayments are financed by reductions in public spending, because this leads to a lack of public demand. In periods of secular stagnation, creditors cannot find any additional real economic investment opportunities. The only remaining solution is to pay the debts using higher taxes, including capital levies.[128]

Because higher taxes and levies would mainly have to be collected from higher earners and the wealthy (if low income earners had to pay them, the rate of consumption would be adversely affected) the rich would ultimately be paying themselves, because they make up the majority of creditors of government debts. See also my discussion of how to prevent adverse effects in the event of capital levies and high inheritance tax on business assets: *Besteuerung des Wirtschaftgeschehens zur Vermeidung einer Neuverschuldung [The Taxation of Economic Activity in Order to Avoid More Borrowing]* in: Unconventional Views on the Economic Crisis II. What Should Be Done to Resolve the Crisis?, page 50ff.

The more the market is emptied of government bonds the better. It is important to realise that debt reduction, for the various reasons outlined, will ultimately have to be financed primarily by the same people who are also the creditors of government debt, whether it happens in this generation or the next. So all the foolish talk about how we must not burden future generations with present government debts in fact makes no sense. Because the creditors of government bonds are also part of the next generation and will, simply put, have to pay back the debts to themselves.[129]

---

[128] See also: Petersen: *Eine Solonische Entschuldung der öffentlichen Hände [The Wisdom of Relieving Public Debt]*, in: Wirtschaftskrise Von Haien, Heuschrecken und anderem Getier [Economic Crisis: Of Sharks, Locusts and Other Animals], Page 109ff and Petersen: *Die Verhinderung und Rückführung zu starker Vermögens- und Einkommensunterschiede [The Prevention and Reversal of Excessive Wealth and Income Disparities]* in: Unconventional Views on the Economic Crisis II. What Should Be Done To Resolve the Crisis? Page 50ff.

[129] See also: Petersen. *Die gespaltene Generation [The Divided Generation]* in: loc.cit., Page 65.

2. Banking regulation

When the causes of the economic crisis are discussed, the real blame is usually placed on the banks and on the politicians, because they liberalised the banking sector again and again, and particularly because they allowed the banks to create more and more credit. A landmark decision, now considered to have been a mistake, was the repeal of the *Glass-Steagall Act* by the then US president Bill Clinton, at the request of Alan Greenspan, then Chairman of the Federal Reserve. The Glass-Steagall Act separated commercial and investment banking, so that private savings and bank deposits could not be used to finance speculative investment.

Criticisms of the deregulation of the banking sector overlooked the fact that it was designed, in keeping with supply-oriented economic policy, to boost banks' business activity, and that easier access to credit was intended to encourage investment by investors and companies. These objectives were both achieved. This encouraged real estate speculation and prevented the American economic growth triggered by the property boom, which had spilled over into the global economy as a whole, from collapsing. In light of the above, it contributed to the *burning* of surplus capital and thereby prevented an economic and global economic demand gap.

If the banking sector is now subjected to stricter regulation once more, the burning of capital will be impeded, and this will encourage economic stagnation and deflation. If we call for stricter regulation of banks without taking any other measures to ensure that national and international economic demand is brought in line with supply opportunities, we should not be surprised when prices do not rise and central banks fear deflation. Anyone who remains committed to supply-oriented economic policy and rejects alternative methods of increasing demand (like public spending, for example) must accept speculation and its collapse as normal economic cycles, and must therefore continue to encourage speculation.

They must live by the economic policy motto 'bring on the bubbles!', which K. Singer used to describe the ideas of Krugman and Summers when he wrote: 'Summers' idea, according to which the world is in danger of descending into secular stagnation, was enthusiastically praised by Nobel Prize winner Krugman. In light of this danger, Summers touts asset price bubbles as being not only inevitable but desirable. And Krugman, the prize winner, cheers him on.' Krugman and Summers see the world as being caught in a liquidity trap. According to Summers, the bubbles that have repeatedly emerged ever since the later years of the Reagan administration are necessary in order to keep the economy at a level close to that of full employment.'[130]

As our experience of the last crisis demonstrates, the crises that come in the wake of speculation have such a devastatingly destructive effect on the economy that they more than undo any economic recovery generated by that speculation. This is why Singer deems the bubble hypothesis to be 'perverse logic', and comments: 'One *key fundamental problem is that the credit system has been completely infected by speculation.* This problem has not yet been eliminated and renders the fantasy of beneficent price bubbles particularly dangerous. What is the point of full employment almost having been achieved during the recent house price bubble, only for all the wealth it created to then be wiped out in the ensuing crash? The crash disproportionately affected earners in middle and below-average income brackets, who did not have enough cash reserves to absorb the impact of the crisis.'[131]

Singer, quite rightly, does not believe that encouraging bubbles is a way of stimulating economic recovery anyway. He writes: 'If capital efficiency decreases in a clear and lasting way, companies no longer invest to the extent that would be needed to support growth. For one thing, managers, investors and Wall Street all have short-term and profit-oriented incentives. Secondly, however (and more importantly): In a *balance sheet recession* the private sector, both businesses and households, reduces its debts, which is equivalent to saving. This sets off a deflationary process. Lower interest rates do not initially have any effect on this. Any attempt to induce inflation under these circumstances is more likely to in-

---

[130] K.Singer: *Blasen her! [Bring on the Bubbles!]* http://www.timepatternanalysis.de/Blog/2013/11/27/blasen-her/
[131] K. Singer: loc. cit.

crease uncertainty in the private sector about future economic development, leading it to cut back its real spending and thereby weakening economic activity still further.[132]

These remarks are not intended as arguments against political initiatives to stabilise the banking system. They are merely designed to illustrate that banking regulation alone is not a solution; it only prevents the burning of capital and thus actually makes secular stagnation worse.[133]

3. Regulation of the money market

From economic experiences since the 1980s and the arguments set out above, it becomes clear that, contrary to classical economic theory, not only does having too much money in circulation trigger inflation: it is also a deciding factor in who is able to use that money as purchasing power. Only when the money is in the hands of consumers or investors in the real economy does it translate into demand and lead, if this causes economic demand to exceed supply, to inflationary price increases. If, however, due to national and/or international competition, employees cannot increase their wages, or cannot increase them above the level of rising productivity, demand will not rise. If wage increases are even lower than increases in productivity, the demand gap actually expands even further in periods of secular stagnation, despite an expanding money supply. During these periods, businesses cannot find enough profitable real economic investment opportunities for their increased profits. The surplus money which is pumped into the economic cycle can then only be used for speculative purposes and the prices of shares and of traded stocks such as property, gold etc. go up.

---

[132] loc. cit.

[133] For more detail see: *Können Weltwirtschaftskrisen durch eine restriktivere Regulierung der Bankgeschäfte verhindert werden? [Can Global Economic Crises be Prevented by More Restrictive Banking Regulation?]* in: Petersen: Unkonventionelle Betrachtungsweisen zur Wirtschaftskrise: Von Haien, Heuschrecken und anderem Getier. [Unconventional Views on the Economic Crisis: On Sharks, Locusts and Other Animals]. Verlag Peter Lang 2011, p. 103ff.

Although prices do not necessarily have to rise when there is economic growth, since according to Say's Law the incomes that purchase products rise along with production, supply-oriented economic policymakers do expect to see rising prices in a boom. They assume that the passion for investment runs so high that the demand for capital will exceed savings.

In periods of secular stagnation, however, this is only ever to be expected in the event of exuberant speculation in real estate or, as happened with the *dotcom bubble*, in new *start-ups*. Generally in times of secular stagnation the supply of savings capital is large enough to enable adequate growth without the general price level having to rise.

Pseudo-inflation can occur, of course, when economic growth or speculation cause increases in the prices of energy and raw materials, which as a result of there being too little downward price elasticity are not offset by reductions in the prices of other goods.[134]

But even when general price rises are the direct result of wage increases, which companies then pass on to consumers in the form of price rises - in other words, when there is cost inflation due to wage-price spirals - it should not be assumed that stagnation has been overcome. As was demonstrated by the period of stagflation leading up to the 1980s, cost inflation and stagnation are not mutually exclusive.

Based on past experiences, particularly over the last ten years, we need to rethink the correlation between inflation and economic booms. These experiences have already led to the money supply from central banks being expanded without reference to the real economy's liquidity requirement, so that it ended up financing only capital market transactions.

---

[134] Such price rises simply reflect the relative scarcity of certain raw materials or foodstuffs, which is then compensated for by targeted increases in production on better harvests. Because central banks do not distinguish between general price rises and rises in the prices of increasingly scarce goods, which also drive up the general price level, they even used such structural price rises as grounds for raising interest rates, though they must have known that they could not lower the prices of existing goods using monetary policy measures without endangering the economy.

If we believe that it is possible to stimulate the economy by adhering to the supply-oriented maxim 'bring on the bubbles!', then we should continue the practice the central banks have hitherto adopted, of flooding the economy with money again and again and showing themselves willing to buy up unlimited amounts of the government bonds of individual countries threatened with bankruptcy. However, if we recognise that the central banks cannot stimulate the real economy with low interest rates and money gluts, we should not go back to current monetary policy.

The task of the central banks is to provide the economy with sufficient liquidity. The greater the liquidity requirement for capital market transactions, the more money there has to be in circulation, naturally, because as a result of the high profits that can be earned through capital market transactions, the real economy is only granted credit once the capital market's borrowing requirements have been met.

Because a plentiful circulation of money encourages speculation, not least in currencies, and because this entails considerable risks for the real economy, as much money as possible should be removed from the capital market. In order to do this, it is advisable that we take the important step of reducing the number of government bonds (which have no material value anyway) in circulation and introduce stricter regulation of the banking sector.

As long as so many government bonds remain in circulation and nations continue to have large amounts of public debt, the European Central Bank's purchase guarantee for old loans must remain in place so that speculation against individual countries does not develop into a conflagration. The purchase guarantee should not apply to new debts, however. If it did, it would tempt ailing countries to keep refinancing themselves on the capital market, thus profiting from the European Central Bank's guarantee.

In April 2014, for example, Greece placed new bonds on the capital market at an interest rate of 4.75%. Ultimately all the countries in the Eurozone are liable for these bonds. This can also lead to rises in interest rates for other countries. If a country like Greece needs to borrow more, and this is recognised by the jointly liable countries of the Eurozone, then Greece should be able to borrow directly from the ECB, at zero interest if possible, so that speculative investors do not profit from the process. However, if a country like Greece takes out new loans on the capital market without the approval of the rest of the countries in the single currency area, the ECB should not issue any purchase guarantee.

Up to now, such direct purchases of government bonds by the Central Bank has been rejected as inadmissible public finance by the state bank. But as long as the Central Bank is independent and is granting these loans for the purpose of supplying money to the economy, the economy should preferably be supplied with money through direct loans to nations. This would prevent
- more government bonds circulating on the capital market
- high interest rates for governments
- speculators profiting from money creation by the ECB

I offer more detailed suggestions in: *Die Sanierung des Geldmarktes [Rehabilitating the Money Market]* in: Unconventional Views on the Economic Crisis II. What Should Be Done To Resolve the Crisis? Page 86ff.

IV. Limitations of globalisation

The international division of labour and international cooperation not only promote prosperity and enrich our lives, they also bring people and cultures together and contribute to world peace. But the globalisation of the economy also levels out regional differences, on the one hand, and on the other hand leads to the concentration of industry and services in particular locations, and thus to an undifferentiated economic structure in less-developed locations.

In the traditional industrialised nations it began with an exodus from rural areas, caused by the huge social and economic differences between cities and the countryside. We have seen that the globalisation of the economy may have accelerated economic development in all countries, but that more developed countries have benefited more from that development than less developed ones. Unchecked economic globalisation has led, moreover, to the emergence of international centres of power controlled by private interests and capable of destroying general prosperity and ultimately the economy as well.

So as to limit the adverse effects of globalisation, and to prevent social and political tensions developing between countries, it is vital to make sure that political systems of governance are maintained. It is necessary, therefore, that economic and political regions join forces so as not to leave countries at the mercy of global economic competition, and to stop them becoming the pawns of speculators. International economic communities need effective political structures, however. Mechanisms and rules should be developed in order to guarantee harmonious joint development and to compensate for the economic disadvantages of individual regions. Countries with a higher concentration of industry or administrative and financial centres, which have higher tax revenues at their disposal, need to give over a proportion of their revenues to less developed regions.

In the structuring of economic communities it is also important to take into account that in addition to a country's stage of industrial development, market size is a deciding factor in economic development. The fact that many international companies invest in China and set up branches there is ultimately thanks to its market size: in other words, its potential for demand. In the traditional industrialised nations, consumer demand based on purchasing power is largely saturated. Given the choice, therefore, companies tend to invest in China rather than in Europe - even if the production conditions (the skill level of the workforce, for example) are not so favourable and the production costs for high-tech production are higher there despite lower wage costs. This must be taken into account when, for instance, we bemoan the fact that in the German Länder of the former GDR industrial development is not making much progress, and even more so, of course, when we think about how to promote the development of southern European countries.

We have already touched upon the fallacy that some countries are characterised by high intelligence and other countries by manual labour, and the fact that it is not desirable that skilled workers should emigrate from developing countries to industrialised ones. Within a society, all sorts of different people should be able to find jobs.

Just as developing countries have introduced foreign trade barriers to ensure they do not degenerate into nothing more than workbenches and commodity-producing countries, so the industrialised countries must ensure that less qualified workers are also able to find paid jobs and that vital industries, such as agriculture, do not disappear. In order to develop relatively less developed regions in Europe, for example, the European market needs to be properly protected by targeted tariff barriers. Just as research and development and technological enterprises in developing countries need to advance and grow, so too must we ensure the economic survival of labour-intensive operations in Europe. This would, of course, render the manufacturing of individual components and their exchange across continents less efficient and generate less profit for global players, but it would be much more likely to lead to harmonious economies and societies in all countries and probably to greater employment as well.

Globalisation also gives multinational companies the ability to freely determine where their headquarters will be - the place where they will record the most profit and where they will domicile their operations - and to change it whenever a more attractive opportunity arises. In this way they avoid taxes and gain financial advantages over businesses which are tied to particular regions, which has nothing to do with fair market competition. And not only this - they are also able, simply by passing a management board resolution, to close down operations which may be of vital importance to a particular region, or to relocate those operations to other countries, potentially because they can obtain subsidies or tax advantages there.

And using clever capital market transactions, corporations can also be bought up, cannibalised and relocated. The way in which hedge funds and shrewd corporate traders buy up and exploit firms is often impossible to understand according to real economic logic, and only serves the purpose of making short-term profits for those who play the capital market.[135] One need only look at the attempt

---

[135] For more detail see: *Die Verwandlung der unternehmerischen Leistungsträger von großen Tieren zu Schmeißfliegen des Kapitalmarktes* [*The Transformation of Service Providers from the Big Fish to the Blowflies of the Capital Market*], in: Petersen: Unkonventionelle Betrachtungsweisen zur Wirtschaftskrise: Von Haien, Heuschrecken und anderem Getier. [Unconventional Views on the Economic Crisis: On Sharks, Locusts and Other Animals].

by Porsche's shareholders to take over the financially much stronger Volkswagen group, and many other similar takeovers which only come about as a result of the possibilities offered by the capital market; possibilities which are hostile to the real economy. It is absurd, too, that hedge funds are able to buy up a country's worthless government bonds (as in Argentina's case) then stand in the way of debt relief for that country, and still expect to make huge profits.

States and regions must defend themselves against such manipulation. Ultimately, building and sustaining economies is a joint effort on the part of communities and must not be abandoned to the speculative interests of those who play the capital market. At the same time, states must work to ensure that chronic export surpluses and corresponding import surpluses do not give rise to global economic imbalances capable of destabilising the global economy.

In order to achieve these objectives, export surpluses should be reduced and companies and business operations, and their revenues, should be anchored more within regions. This could be achieved by taking the following measures:
- reducing export and import surpluses
- ensuring better assignment of profit to operating facilities
- employee participation
- state investment

1. Reducing export and import surpluses

Capital export as a result of export surpluses means either
- debt incurred by import surplus countries and thus increased potential for speculation, or
- the relocation of operations from export surplus countries to other countries.

Where export surpluses are not financed through deliberate capital export for investment or other expenditure abroad, the consequence is an increase in the level of foreign debt of import surplus countries. Because they fund investments which promote the development of the real economy in import surplus countries, these import surpluses can be very welcome. But if these investments lead to the destruction of traditional manufacturing, the unemployment rate in the importing countries can rise, which is why it is advisable under certain circumstances to use import barriers to protect certain economic areas. Chronic import surpluses mean, however, that not enough is being produced domestically and correspondingly that there are too few people in employment - the jobs are going to the people who are producing goods for export in the export surplus countries.

Even more problematic are the import surpluses which are funded by foreign loans for state consumption. The higher national debt climbs, the greater the danger that the country will become an object of speculation, become devalued as an economic location and in some cases be driven to the point of national bankruptcy when new loans are refused.

On the other hand, the export surplus countries not only have to bear the risk that loans will not be repaid - they can also get into difficulty when loans are repaid, because this reduces capital export and widens the demand gap in the export surplus country itself. It is the export surplus countries' dependence on capital export in order to close the domestic demand gap which makes it so difficult to get rid of chronic export surpluses. Because in secular stagnation the import surplus countries cannot combat the most powerful industries in the export surplus countries, as long as demand there is not growing, the balance of trade can only be levelled out by production being transferred from the export surplus countries to the import surplus countries. If this solution is rejected, the only other option is to siphon off the surplus savings in the export surplus countries through higher wages and use them to increase state spending and to increase economic demand.

2. Better assignment of profit to operating facilities to ensure appropriate taxation

One major reason why taxes worldwide have been reduced so sharply, even for high earners, is that international competition enables countries to tempts companies and wealthy individuals abroad by offering lower taxes. Often all a country has to do is make sure that these companies and individuals channel their profits through it, simply by setting up *holdings, licensing firms, commercial agencies* etc., which are often just letterbox companies.

It is not only important financial centres like London, Wall Street in New York, Switzerland, Luxembourg and various tax havens that live off capital transfer. Countries like Ireland, which has a flat corporate tax rate of only 12.5%, have also attracted many firms this way.

Because a business is a joint effort on the part of employers, employees, investors and those who contribute their know-how, but provides its service in a particular place, this sort of profit transfer is unjustified. This is why these loopholes need to be closed. Within the European Community, minimum tax standards need to be laid down and procedures developed for flight capital to enable cross-border profits to be assigned to the operations which are providing the service. This will be no easy task, undoubtedly, and can only be addressed on a longer term basis. A few years ago it was inconceivable that tax havens could ever be induced to give up fiscal secrets to other tax authorities. If necessary, transfers made for the purposes of tax avoidance must be combated through discrimination against imports from these countries and through other trade tariff measures or capital market restrictions.

One way of making sure taxes were paid in the places where operations were based would be to develop and focus more on trade tax. From a supply-oriented perspective, taxing earnings primarily targets individual incomes. For this reason, liberal economic policymakers are always attempting to abolish trade tax. But 'trade tax', as Wikipedia states, 'is levied on the objective profitability of a commercial enterprise.'[136] Because economies are a joint effort by employers, investors and employees, however, trade tax should be the primary tax and income tax the secondary tax.

With regard to trade tax, all costs that come out of operating profit in the form of licenses, profit sharing or interest and are not subject to trade tax themselves for the recipients should be treated as incomes. Where equity links exist - including to foreign countries - operating facilities must be assigned an appropriate share in profits, to be determined on the basis of trade taxes.

---

[136]

http://de.wikipedia.org/wiki/Gewerbesteuer_%28Deutschland%29#Aktuelle_Reformvorschl.C3.A4ge

In this way we can combat the transfer of profits to regions offering tax advantages. As long as municipalities retain the right to choose the level of real estate tax they levy, the basic tax rate must be high enough for profit transfers not to be worthwhile.

The higher trade tax is set, the lower profit taxation, such as corporation tax and capital gains tax, can be. Paid trade tax could also be deducted from income tax statements. But when implementing such a reform it is important to ensure there is no exodus, and if necessary trade taxes must be accompanied by other foreign economic policy measures.

3. Empowering employees in order to protect jobs

In times of hardship or rationalisation in order to increase profit, companies often close down operating facilities. In the case of large sites this can lead not only to unemployment for the affected employees but also to a severe weakening of the economic power of individual regions and countries. For the workers who have been laid off, this can mean that they are unable to find alternative employment. This danger is particularly great in periods of secular stagnation, of course.

In such cases - the closing of the Opel plants or the Nokia plant in Bochum, for example, and the relocation of production to Romania - it is usually not just trade unions but also national governments who intervene and try to avert the implications this would have for jobs and for regions. Usually, however, all that can be offered to the owners of a company is subsidies, and workers accepting wage cuts. This may still not be enough for the company, and it may close down sites or make swingeing job cuts regardless.

In order to combat this, employees should be given more of an opportunity to be involved in business decisions. The most important thing is not to increase shareholders' profits but to ensure secure jobs for employees. Naturally, jobs cannot be maintained in the face of adverse market developments. But giving staff more power to participate in decisions could make it easier to find alternatives. Jusy look at Opel! If the employees had been more involved in business planning, the German Opel plants might not have closed because the employees would have pushed for Opel to be given the right to export to Eastern Europe, which it had not been allowed to do until then because the parent company General Motors had earmarked the Eastern European market for itself. It might also have been possible to offer the sites to other car manufacturers. Given the employees' high level of production know-how, this might have been an attractive proposition for Asian car manufacturers wanting to get a foothold in the European market.

4. More state investment to fund collective needs and to prevent the unnecessary relocation of operations

The needs of a population cannot be organised centrally by a public administration. This is why all centrally planned economies have failed in the end. However, collective needs and infrastructure investment are best financed and carried out by public entities. If roads, schools etc. were built and operated purely on the basis of the private sector's profit motive there would be too little consideration of the public interest, as has been made clear by public discussions regarding water and energy supplies and private schools and universities. This is unless private initiatives and the public interest are aligned with one another to some extent: for example, toll roads, energy networks, publicly financed private schools etc. are subject to targets, price limits and in the case of private schools, the obligation to admit a sufficient number of children from low-income families.

Before globalisation, employers and holders of capital within a national economy were largely one and the same people, and because they were bound to their location they were more inclined to do things that were of benefit to the community. Employers and employees shared a common interest in their collaborative work.

Globalisation has changed all that. Production and distribution are increasingly being usurped by international corporations, and holders of capital no longer invest in companies they know and to which they feel some kind of emotional connection. Instead they invest on the international capital market, in more or less anonymous capital market securities.

The fate of a business and its workers interests international institutional investors only as far as generating the maximum short-term profit is concerned. The majority of such profit comes not from dividends but from share price rises.

Infrastructure investments can also require such vast sums that they cannot possibly be privately financed. Basic research, for example, is made possible by generous grants from the public purse. Huge undertakings like the provision of an environmentally sound energy supply can hardly be tackled by private companies, because what would the goals have to be: a broad supply of wind, solar, hydroelectric and geo-energy and energy from renewable materials. The required distribution network would preferably need to be laid underground.

As the politicians' hopeless attempts testify, this is ultimately only possible through public organisation with a massive amount of lost subsidies. The conversion of the energy supply and other important collective needs must be financed by higher levies on the income of those whose needs are already satisfied and who use their surplus savings merely to play the capital market.

Funds collected in this way will be turned back into real economic demand, thereby stimulating the economy. It will no longer be necessary for so much capital to be exported and the import opportunities for foreign countries will improve.

Also, given that a balanced employment structure within a given region is so clearly in the public interest, we must ensure that vital businesses do not simply disappear because they have been bought up and cannibalised by competitors or financial locusts. Regions must therefore be given the right to proclaim core competencies for their areas and to acquire interests in businesses which are vital to them, in order to prevent workers being dismissed unnecessarily .

The Volkswagen Law could serve as an example. If the state of Lower Saxony had not had a share and a qualified codetermination in the Volkswagen group, it might already have been bought up by international capital funds, leaving it at the mercy of external speculators. Porsche's unsuccessful attempt to buy the VW group using hedge fund money shows how easily this can happen. Crucially, this attempt was blocked by Lower Saxony's veto.

Of course, there is no point in continuing to produce things that can no longer be sold. But when restructuring is needed, decisive state intervention can be helpful.[137]

---

[137] See also: Petersen. *Brauchen wir eine weitere Privatisierung oder eher eine stärkere Resozialisierung von Wirtschaftsunternehmen? [Do*

D. Criteria of secular stagnation and necessary economic policy measures

Criteria for secular stagnation are:
1. Criterion: higher savings than there are lucrative private sector investment opportunities in the real economy
2. Criterion: extreme inequality in the distribution of income and wealth
3. very low interest rates
4. rising property prices due to increasing pressure to invest
5. an extremely uneven balance of foreign trade

I. Criterion: Higher savings than there are lucrative private sector investment opportunities in the real economy

When savings outstrip real economic investments, an economy will shrink until the savings have been turned back into investments. These days, the cause of this imbalance is the consumption saturation points of those earners with purchasing power - high earners in particular.

In a situation like this, supply-oriented economic policy measures no longer succeed in stimulating economic growth, only speculation (at best). The only viable options are to increase consumption by strengthening the purchasing power of low-income earners, and to increase state spending. To stop public debt rising any further, however, public expenditure must be financed solely by higher revenues.

We Need More Privatisation Or More Re-socialising of Companies?] in: Unconventional... On Sharks, Locusts and Other Animals, page 113ff.

II. Criterion: extreme inequality in the distribution of income and wealth

In a less developed economy, unequal income distribution can stimulate economic growth because consumer demand is still underdeveloped and so it is easier to fund investment using savings. In the developed economies, on the other hand, extreme inequality in the distribution of wealth - which in turn leads to unequal income distribution - is a sign of secular stagnation, because profitable investments are unlikely to keep pace with rising national income and corresponding increases in the volume of savings.

III. Criterion: very low interest rates.

The interest rates in the industrialised nations are currently so low that monetary policy measures to boost the economy are failing. Increases in the money supply by central banks can no longer even induce inflation, because the additional supply of money does not end up in the hands of those who would use it to buy more consumer goods; this also means it is no longer worthwhile making any investments.

If workers were able to push through wage increases in spite of this, they would not only be endangering their own jobs - companies would also pass on the increase in costs to consumers, in the form of price rises. We would then end up with *stagflation*, i.e. stagnation plus rising prices.

Expansionary monetary policy too, then, is capable only of encouraging people to play the capital market.

The only remedies for excessively low interest rates are:
- to dry out the capital market as much as possible through higher repayments of public debts financed by higher taxes and levies, particularly from those who hold the capital market securities.
- to make capital market transactions more difficult using taxes on capital transfers and regulations on banks and the capital market.

IV. Rising property prices due to increasing pressure to invest

What characterises a feudal economy is a situation in which land is owned by the nobility, and ground rents are paid to them - in former times peasants had to pay tithes to the nobility comprising one-tenth of the harvest. While the power relations in those days may have been appropriate to the historical conditions, from the point of view of modern working conditions the nobles were parasites, leading luxurious lives on the backs of their subordinates.

In urban craftsmen's workshops, people's own output was their main source of income. In capitalism it was initially employers who commanded the most income, as increasing productive forces brought them increases in capital income.

The heirs of those who had acquired the productive capital then resumed the role of feudal pensioners as soon as they received the returns on the capital. Only if they also worked themselves did they take any part in working life.

Ownership of productive capital differs from ownership of property and particularly of land, however, in the sense that productive capital only has value for as long as it can be used to produce goods and services. It also wears out over the course of the production process and has to be replaced over and over again. Property and particularly land, on the other hand, have lasting value - although the price of land depends on what that land can be used for. Pasture land and plots in shopping streets, for example, are worth very different amounts. But everyone does consider land ownership as a secure capital investment, whatever might happen economically.

This is why real estate is a favourite object of speculation. Particularly in times of secular stagnation, during which investment opportunities in the real economy are limited and interest rates are low, investors flock to real estate.

One fatal side effect of the low interest rate policy in times of secular stagnation is that according to the rules of short-term capital optimisation, real estate is seen as undervalued in comparison to other investment opportunities, meaning it can rise considerably in price. When there is a prospect of such price increases, players of the capital market - who are primarily concerned with short-term price increases - are on the spot, ready to try to sell again at the right time and profit from the differences in prices. In this way housing estates, for example, can be passed on repeatedly from one owner company to the next.

Due to the pressure to invest in conjunction with investors playing the capital market, the price of real estate can be driven so high that returns fall below the level of returns on other, comparable capital investments. This then leads to rents being raised and thus helps shift more purchasing power from renters, who tend to be on lower incomes, over to capital investors.

This development is encouraged by the fact that the property market does not fully adhere to the optimal principles of the market. Furthermore, it is dominated by large corporations and given the choice, landlords sometimes leave rooms standing empty, as experience has shown. This is why the property market is also particularly subject to possible forms of state influence.

If there are enough real economic investment opportunities and attractive interest rates are paid on savings, the danger of property bubbles is small. Conversely, if property prices rise steeply when interest rates are low, this is also a criterion of secular stagnation.

V. Criterion: uneven balance of foreign trade

Another unmistakeable sign of secular stagnation is a chronically uneven foreign trade balance. This is because chronically active foreign trade balances have a correspondingly large net capital export surplus and this means that domestic purchasing power cannot be exercised sufficiently within a country, so that the savings in question have to be transferred abroad. The cause of this, aside from a high level of saturation in more developed economies, is usually extreme inequality in income and wealth distribution.

As long as foreign trade surpluses exist, a country can fancy itself to have a thriving economy, but this only takes into account its high employment rate relative to other countries, and not the relative impoverishment of the less well-off within its own population.

An active foreign trade balance, moreover, is no guarantee of low unemployment. Workers may in fact have been made redundant and replaced by machines, computers and robots. An economy with growing export surpluses can grow in spite of this. But the additional economic growth generated in this way flows predominantly to holders of capital and to executives.

High chronic export surpluses naturally make a country extremely dependent on other countries. If export surpluses fall away or even if they just decrease, then the capital which is no longer being exported abroad must be spent domestically, which is unlikely to happen. This is because, as export opportunities shrink, hardly any companies will continue to invest domestically; instead, they will restrict their investments even further and thus exacerbate the demand shortage. And it is also unlikely that holders of capital will start to consume more. The disappearance of export surpluses will therefore drive the economy of an export surplus country into depression.

And in the course of capital export more jobs may be transferred abroad than are emerging at home. When production is relocated abroad and jobs arise domestically in compensation, they are usually only associated with handling activities. But because handling activities are increasingly carried out with the aid of computers and machines, what usually happens is simply that a larger workload falls to the existing handling staff, so that, at most, their salaries go up. In other words, capital export can also result in deindustrialisation, another sign of secular stagnation

As a consequence of deindustrialisation, the export surplus could be reduced and even give way to an import surplus. This need not affect holders of capital. They then just obtain more of their profit from abroad and import the consumer goods they need from abroad. Import surpluses with corresponding capital imports are thus an even more dangerous form of secular stagnation. The places worst affected are less developed economies with a rich elite which has invested its money abroad and imports whatever consumer goods it requires. So the capital imports of countries which used to have large colonies are also likely to be the result of income from foreign assets.

Even more concerning, however, are import surpluses financed by high national debt. The higher national debt is, the greater the danger that countries will be unable to pay it, with attendant consequences not only for the economies of those countries but also for the global economy.

E. How economic policy is still only treating the economy's symptoms and this is increasing its susceptibility to crises, as illustrated by the Merkel government.

After the last war, the USA dominated the global economy. When America was in financial trouble, it was felt by the rest of the world too. It was said of the economy that 'when America sneezes, the world catches a cold'. The USA's dominant position persists to this day, but has been relativised by the development of other economic centres with the result that the global economy is now also dependent on the economic health of these other centres.

One of these new centres is Europe and, as the strongest economic power in Europe, Germany. In the past, the USA was called upon to be aware of its importance for the global economy as a whole and accordingly to act in a responsible manner; now this demand is also applied to Europe, and within Europe particularly to Germany.

The Merkel government, however, does not seem to be fully cognisant of this responsibility. Still caught in the trap of a supply-oriented ideology, and with little or no understanding of the special economic conditions prevailing in times of secular stagnation, it thinks that the real economic problems lie in excessive national debts and the deregulation of the capital market. It does not even question why public debt has risen so high, and what the significance of borrowing has been for economic development up to now, and why the commercial activities of banks were deregulated.

Aside from this, the Merkel government puts its trust in entrepreneurial activity and the 'self-healing' powers of the market, except where the energy market is concerned, and other market effects that are detrimental to German industry.

The Merkel government feels itself to be justified in its economic policy by the fact that Germany is flourishing economically in comparison to the rest of the world. It does not see, however, that this flourishing is dependent upon export surpluses and attendant capital export surpluses - in other words, on other countries' import surpluses. Because all the criteria of secular stagnation that have already been listed

1. higher savings than there are lucrative private sector investment opportunities in the real economy
2. extreme inequality in the distribution of income and wealth
3. very low interest rates
4. rising property prices due to increasing pressure to invest
5. an extremely uneven balance of foreign trade

are applicable to Germany. Germany serves as a particularly clear example of how economic policy which is still in thrall to the supply-oriented economic ideology merely treats the symptoms of secular stagnation, thus rendering the economy more vulnerable to crises.

I. How the Merkel government's economic and taxation policies are not reducing export surpluses and are thereby increasing the economy's susceptibility to crises.

While almost all countries, but particularly the more developed ones, are suffering from high unemployment and signs of depression, Germany is seen as the happy exception and even as a role model for how to overcome economic problems.

But the global economy is like a system of communicating pipes and since Germany is obviously also part of the global economy, its strengths are other countries' weaknesses. If the other countries were to be destroyed by these weaknesses, this would also rebound on Germany and endanger Germany's economic stability. Germany would even find itself in economic trouble if other countries were to reduce their import surpluses (which are Germany's export surpluses), because if that happened, there would no longer be enough export surpluses in the German economy's supply/demand balance to offset excess savings.

Other countries are increasingly - and quite rightly - beginning to complain about German export surpluses, which plunge these countries further into debt and reduce the number of people they are able to employ (in correlation to their import surpluses). In other words, there is a lack of jobs in the import surplus countries equivalent to the number of jobs that are retained in Germany as a result of export surpluses.

Holger Zschäpitz writes: 'In Davos [2014], Germany came in for a certain amount of criticism. Time and time again it was said that stubborn adherence to the stability policy could plunge the Eurozone into deflation or even depression. Almost unanimously, Berlin was called upon to grant the European Central Bank more leeway to halt such a fatal downward spiral.'[138] This is why Germany, even within the EU, is in the dock.

This issue has been brushed under the carpet by German economic policymakers, because they take it for granted that the performance of the southern Member States will improve. It is hoped that these countries will become much more industrialised. But this hope has been dashed before, in relation to the former GDR after German reunification, despite the fact that the GDR was already an industrialised nation. Faced with the highly developed industrial potential, know-how and market position of the Federal Republic, the companies of the former GDR had no chance, and following reunification they were liquidated one after another. In this respect we might as well give up on this hope in relation to the southern Member States too. German companies are unlikely to relocate production on a significant scale to Greece, for example. When German companies expand they go to emerging countries, which not only offer lower labour costs but also enormous sales potential.

All that is left, therefore, is consumer goods and tourism services. In these areas the services provided by these countries to others could certainly be increased. However, this is unlikely to have a direct impact on German export surpluses, because it will not cause the 80% of German earners who receive only around 40% of national income to increase their level of consumption. In any case, bringing in more goods from other Eurozone countries

---

[138] Holger Zschäpitz, Davos: *Deflationsgefahr. Geldhistoriker warnt vor fataler Abwärtsspirale [Deflation Risk. Economic Historian Warns of Fatal Downward Spiral]*. DIE WELT 24/01/14,
http://www.welt.de/finanzen/article124170432/Geldhistoriker-warnt-vor-fataler-Abwaertsspirale.html

would happen at the expense of goods and services from non-Eurozone countries. The Germans would then buy more oranges and vegetables from Greece, for example, instead of from Israel and Morocco, and would visit more beaches in Greece than in Turkey. On balance, however, German consumption would not increase and so Germany's export surpluses would not be reduced. The growing foreign debt resulting from the export surpluses would then affect more non-European countries. On a global scale, the susceptibility to crises would not be lessened.

At most, improvements in the current account balances of the southern Member States would be reflected in the exchange rate value of the euro; if southern European countries start exporting more and by exporting to other European countries they effect a reduction in the amount of imports from non-European countries, the price of the euro will rise and German exports will be impeded. This would adversely affect the economy and the employment rate in Germany.

It is impossible to clearly predict whether and to what extent rises in the exchange rate value of the euro might reduce the quantity of German exports. At all events, the exchange rate fluctuations in the value of the euro in recent years have hardly had any impact on export surpluses. The demand for high quality German industrial facilities, mainly from emerging countries, might also be so high that other countries would accept higher prices. If imports did not then rise to the same extent, the export surplus and thus the debt of non-European countries would even tend to rise and further reductions in the price of imported goods from outside Europe would in turn affect the southern Member States. For as long as we are unable to increase consumption in Germany, either the export surplus will remain in place or the employment rate will drop.

Maintaining the current level of German export surpluses and attendant import surpluses in other countries would keep increasing the risk of a crisis, which would also have implications for Germany. The German economy may be sitting pretty with its export surpluses at the moment, but it has not overcome secular stagnation - its export surpluses are only preventing or postponing the outbreak of depression in its own country at the expense of other countries.

But how could export surpluses be eliminated? Export bans are out of the question. They would lead directly to higher unemployment, given that there are no alternative sales outlets to be found in Germany in periods of secular stagnation. In the medium term German companies would be forced to relocate production of the goods in question abroad, without there being any likelihood of new production starting up in Germany - and if it did, it would only lead to more export surpluses. Given its current high rate of savings, after all, there is no way Germany can achieve an even balance of foreign trade without allowing unemployment to rise.

Export surpluses and attendant capital export surpluses can only be eliminated by increasing consumption in Germany so that less money is saved, or more money is invested, and domestic savings are converted into demand. A higher economic consumption rate, however, would only be possible if the wage level were to rise and/or taxes and levies, particularly for higher earners and those with wealth, were to be raised in order to finance public spending.

But both these approaches go against supply-oriented economic doctrine, and as a result there is considerable opposition to them, especially in the ruling CDU. The FDP - the 'guardian' of supply-side economic policies[139] - lost its influence on policy in the 2013 parliamentary election, though the SPD, in its role as new coalition partner of the CDU, has only been able to implement a limited number of economic policy reforms more suited to overcoming secular stagnation. It did, however, manage to bring in a minimum wage.

In terms of increasing wages, in Germany as in other countries, it is not possible to do much more than establish a minimum wage without endangering jobs. Other countries in the Eurozone have forfeited competitiveness in relation to Germany and to third countries as a result. Besides, if wages were increased companies would pass on these extra wage costs to consumers as far as possible, in the form of price rises, and the effects of income redistribution would evaporate. As the earlier discussion of stagflation in the

---

[139] See: Petersen: *Mehr Netto vom Brutto. Das Patentrezept der Liberalen zur Lösung von Wirtschaftsproblemen [More Net From Gross: The Liberals' Panacea for Solving Economic Problems]*, in Unkonventionelle Betrachtungsweisen … I [Unconventional Views...I], page 95ff.

1970s and early 1980s showed, stagnation is not overcome by wage-price spirals. We simply end up with stagnation plus inflation - i.e. *stagflation*.

But by financing pension and healthcare provision, the transport system and support for families, children, education and culture, the burden on employees could be reduced, leaving them with more money for private consumption.

If and to the extent, however, that domestic demand cannot be increased through higher wages, the only option that remains is to spend more money on public investment and the improved fulfilment of public needs, including public housing.

II. How the German social security system encourages secular stagnation

A collective duty, which affects everybody and which calls for a solution based on solidarity, is the provision of unemployment benefits, healthcare and pensions.

As we know, however, responsibility for this task, which affects the vast majority of citizens, is borne solely by working people and by the companies that employ them. People are living longer and longer and the number of people of working age having to fund the pensions of the elderly is growing smaller and smaller. This means that less and less workers (in relative terms) are carrying a higher and higher financial burden, while top income earners on higher incomes are exempt and only have to pay their own health and pension insurance premiums.

Because there is a limit to the burden that can be placed on employees, unemployment benefits and pension incomes, in relation to the provision workers used to receive, are progressively shrinking - in spite of the fact that gross national product is much higher now than it was in the past. How is this possible?

Incomes have risen mainly among those who do not contribute to social security. In addition to increasing incomes from capital investments, capital incomes have risen as jobs have been cut, and companies have also saved on their employee contributions to social security. This is a scandal in terms of both social and economical policy, in the latter case because as a result of having to pay employee contributions, wage-intensive operations are disadvantaged compared to capital-intensive operations. What is to be done?

In an economic order based on solidarity, all earners have an obligation to solve the problem of providing unemployment benefits, healthcare and pensions as a matter of course. In other words, All earners have to make social security contributions, including those on higher incomes and those receiving profit, pensions and capital incomes. If necessary these contributions should be progressive to some extent in line with rising income. In return, everybody would receive basic social security capped at a certain level, which could of course be topped up with additional insurance.

This would end the fraught debate about inadequate unemployment benefits, healthcare costs and pensions. At the same time, higher earners' excess savings would be siphoned off. Tax subsidies would no longer need to be paid for social security and would be available for other forms of public spending.

It would also be preferable to do away with employer contributions to social security if possible, so that labour-intensive operations were no longer disadvantaged in this respect in comparison to capital-intensive operations. This would also eliminate the incentive to save on employer contributions to social security by cutting jobs.

Getting higher earners to contribute to social security could also be argued for from a Christian point of view, but ironically it is the *Christian Democratic Union* which is blocking the switch to a system of basic social security provision

The continuation of the current social security system with its high and rising social security contributions is placing a burden on workers and reducing their ability to consume accordingly. It also means all the money being spent on tax subsidies is unavailable for other forms of public spending. And by burdening labour-intensive operations with employer contributions, it is encouraging businesses to cut jobs and make workers redundant. In this way, the German government's policies are exacerbating secular stagnation.

III. How the Merkel government is exacerbating secular stagnation through insufficient public investment

An effective and efficient public infrastructure is another of our collective needs. Although Germany is seen as an economically prosperous country, it not only has many precarious jobs and increasing old-age poverty but also a public infrastructure which is in desperate condition, with roads, bridges and public buildings sorely in need of renovation.

In Marcel Fratzscher's book *Die Deutschland Illusion [The Germany Illusion]*[140], published on 29/09/2014, Germany's lack of domestic investment, and the way it lags behind that other countries is discussed in detail.

'These days, when Marcel Fratzscher gives a talk', reports Der Spiegel, 'he likes to gives his audience a little riddle to solve. "Which country is this?" asks the head of the German Institute for Economic Research: Since the turn of the millennium it has seen less growth than the average European country. There has been only a slight increase in productivity in its companies, and two out of three workers have a lower income now than in the year 2000.'[141] This country with its weak economic balance sheet is not Portugal or Italy or France, as the audience expects, but Germany.

Another important political mission is the planned transition to energy generation from renewable sources (solar, wind, hydro and geothermal energy) and the use of renewable raw materials, as well as the necessary expansion of the energy grid. The necessary distribution networks will need to be installed underground as far as possible, which entails additional costs.

Fratzscher evidently takes the same view. According to *Der Spiegel*, he believes that: 'If the turnaround in energy policy is successful, it will create a new non-nuclear infrastructure worth many hundreds of billions of Euros. If the project ends in chaos, it may cause damage on a similarly large scale. ...Fratzscher... advocates as radical a move as possible away from the traditional raw materials of coal and oil. In their place he wants us, as soon as possible,

---

[140] Marcel Fratzscher: *Die Deutschland-Illusion*, Hanser Verlag Munich
[141] Alexander Jung et. al.: *Der Scheinriese [The Bogus Giant]*, in: Der Spiegel No. 37, 8/9/2014, p. 63.

to enter an age of solar and wind energy and to set ambitious energy savings targets for property owners and businesses.[142]

Entirely in keeping with classical economic theory, desperate attempts are being made to shift the costs onto German consumers as far as possible. If successful, this would restrict consumers' ability to purchase other goods accordingly. Naturally, the costs cannot be shifted onto businesses either without harming their competitiveness internationally. And businesses, after all, are not responsible for the political decision to revolutionise the energy system. Both these things would only exacerbate secular stagnation. The only other option, therefore, is for the majority of these costs to be publicly financed.

IV. How the Merkel government's taxation policy is exacerbating secular stagnation.

As has been thoroughly demonstrated, demand in Germany can only be usefully and meaningfully increased through higher public spending. The more excess savings are siphoned off, the more the level of economic savings will start to resemble that of real economic investment opportunities - investment will even be stimulated by rising public spending.

Because state spending must not be financed by increased government debt, the only option is to increase public revenue. In the run-up to the last election the *Greens* and the *Left*, but also the *SPD*, made sensible suggestions in this regard. The *CDU*, however, remains the most attached to the outdated neoclassical supply-oriented economic model, so it rejects tax increases and was able to veto them in coalition talks to form a grand coalition with the SPD.

Thanks to Germany's relatively good economic development, tax revenues are so plentiful that they are sufficient to fund the spending laid down in the coalition agreement. But in practice there have been two tax rises. Middle income earners are increas-

---

[142] loc. cit. p. 69.

ingly being pushed into higher tax brackets. Often, the increases in their incomes barely compensate for general price rises. This is known as 'cold progression', or bracket creep.

It means the state does receive more revenue, but not from those people who are saving excessively. These revenues, therefore, are obtained at the expense of private consumption and investment by people who are self-employed. So-called 'cold progression' is felt by all partners to be unfair. And in addition to this, it exacerbates secular stagnation by causing a drop in demand.

V. Insufficient reduction of public debt in order to lessen the economy's susceptibility to crises caused by speculation, and in order to act as a role model for other Eurozone counties.

There is a particularly high risk of crises attached to public debt when the 'markets', as they call them, no longer have confidence that loans granted to individual states will be repaid. This can cause a country's economy to collapse. This has to do not only with additional borrowing but also the refinancing of old debts that fall due. The more links the heavily indebted country has to other countries, the greater the danger that it will pull these other countries into the crisis along with it.

If the USA, for example, which in 2014 has a debt worth 105.7% of gross domestic product[143], were to become insolvent, the whole of the global economy would descend into crisis. This could even happen if the US Senate or Congress were to refuse to raise the debt ceiling (the legal limit how much the US government is allowed to borrow), as has been feared several times over the past few years.

A particularly close interrelationship exists between the Member States of the Eurozone. Furthermore, the public debts of individual states are held for the most part by Eurozone banks, meaning that

---

143

http://de.statista.com/statistik/daten/studie/165786/umfrage/staatsverschuldung-der-usa-in-relation-zum-bruttoinlandsprodukt-bip/

when Greece was deemed insolvent it was not only Greece's economy that was threatened with collapse but also a number of crucial banks within the Eurozone. Economic policymakers also feared that if Greece's insolvency had not been prevented through political measures by the rest of the Eurozone countries and the *International Monetary Fund*, the 'markets' would have lost confidence in the ability of Portugal, Ireland, Italy and Spain to pay their debts, and the entire Eurozone would have been plunged into crisis.

To ward off the danger of such insolvency crises there were calls, crucially from Germany, to enact *debt brakes* in European countries, and in some cases even to enshrine them in national constitutions.

In principle, *debt brakes* are imperative from the point of view of economic policy in order to halt the growth in the number of government bonds in circulation with no material value - we have therefore classified them as *toxic assets*, wholly dependent on the willingness of the 'markets' to keep prolonging them.

But when fixing debt brakes there is too little consideration of the fact that for all the savings which were previously being removed from the market through borrowing, equivalent amounts will need to be additionally invested or burned on the capital market so as to prevent a corresponding widening of the demand gap, which would accelerate secular stagnation. This also applies to the restriction of state spending in order to avoid further borrowing.

This insight has not yet been reflected in German policymaking. Everybody is insisting that no additional debts must be taken on. But where is demand is supposed to come from if state spending is cut too? This is a question that German politics believes it does not need to concern itself with due to its continuing neoclassical mentality.

More European investment support is supposed to be being funnelled into at-risk countries. But for one thing, this support is only a *drop in the ocean* in comparison to the lack of demand on the part of states and the attendant loss of purchasing power experience by the population, and for another thing, who is going to invest more in times of widespread secular stagnation, especially in countries with declining demand?

Because of its relatively good economic development and plentiful tax revenues, Germany has less problems with the prescribed debt brakes and is still not aiming to implement them until after 2015. In the Eurozone countries classed as at risk of insolvency, the programme of debt prevention via spending cuts is leading to such a high level of unemployment that government revenues are falling even further, meaning that in practice they are barely able to comply with the debt brakes.

An increase in global economic demand can only be achieved by siphoning off excess savings and turning them back into demand. In order to do this, public spending on vital public infrastructure and the meeting of collective needs would need to be massively expanded and financed by taxes and levies on those whose needs and real economic investment opportunities are already fulfilled.

If Germany started financing debts and additional public spending using higher revenues, it would be able to put pressure on other Eurozone countries, ones which are heavily in debt, to do the same - in other words, it would be able to get them to raise additional levies on their upper classes who transfer most of their savings abroad.

In view of the extreme inequality that exists in wealth and income distribution, this would probably not affect the standard of living of the upper classes in these countries either. In this way, the debts could be reduced and the economy boosted. (Care should be taken, however, to ensure that additional public spending does not vanish into corrupt structures or perpetuate unhealthy economic conditions.)

We would also see an end to the wretched debate over who is liable for other countries debts. If the upper classes are made to participate in debt reduction - they, after all, are the only ones with the capacity to pay for it - then neither *'bailout funds'* nor the *European Central Bank* will be forced to assume liability for these debts. Where economic policy is concerned we can no longer assume that profit automatically turns into investment; instead national product must be looked at as a whole, and we must ask where there is purchasing power and where it is needed, so that as little profit is left for playing the capital market.

Since public debt can be expected to rise at a higher rate than economic growth, there is no point in continuing to hope that public debt will be generally reduced in relation to gross domestic product as a result of economic growth. There is still a danger, therefore, of speculation against states and currencies. Only through net debt reductions, financed by additional revenues, can the danger of speculation against states be eliminated.

For the economic supply and demand balance, this would mean that higher earners and those with wealth would lose purchasing power as a result of the higher levies but would get it back again in the form of debt repayments. In this way the global balance of supply and demand can be maintained. It is possible, of course, that those asked to bear a heavier burden might not necessarily get back equivalent amounts in the form of debt repayments and that others might get more back than they paid out. But this friction would only be limited, especially since the consumption requirements of the rich and those with assets would not be restricted, and real economic investment opportunities are in short supply as a result of secular stagnation.

Due to its lack of attention to the problems of secular stagnation, the German government is still allowing neoclassical economic ideology to dictate its economic and taxation policies. This is evidenced by the fact that it is doing too little to reduce public debt using additional taxation. Raising taxes is almost a taboo subject for the German government. The fact that other Eurozone countries which are classed as heavily indebted are encouraged to reduce their debts by cutting spending instead of by raising taxes and levies is a product of the same ideology. The German government doubtless believes its policies are making the Eurozone less vulnerable to crises; on balance, however, it is making secular stagnation worse.

VI. The Merkel government's lack of understanding of monetary policy in times of secular stagnation

According to neoclassical economic policy, increasing the money supply over and above the liquidity requirement of the real economy leads to inflation. In order to prevent states increasing their spending too much using loans from central banks and thereby triggering general price increases, central banks are not allowed to grant major loans to public authorities. In the context of its open market policy for the purpose of money supply control, however, a central bank is allowed to buy up government bonds from the capital market.

But in these days of secular stagnation and casino capitalism the money is used primarily to play the capital market, meaning that if there is not enough money available for playing the capital market, there is not enough left for the real economy. For this reason, as long as excess savings have to be burnt on the capital market a high and, if necessary, steadily increasing supply of money is required. When stock exchanges are obliged to report ever higher share prices in order to keep 'the markets' happy, the necessary liquidity has to be made available. If it is not made available and if, as a result, there is not enough liquidity left over for the requirements of the real economy and/or not enough excess savings are being burnt on the capital market, the economy falls into crisis.

From the neoclassical perspective of the Merkel government and the economic researchers who back it, this liquidation of the economy is irresponsible. But if excess savings are not siphoned off, the burning of capital on the capital market is the only way to avoid the outbreak of crises, particularly when states are not able to take on any more debt in order to turn savings back into real economic demand via public spending.

The call for stricter regulation of the capital market is similarly problematic. In itself, it is desirable in order to prevent speculation from disrupting economic activity. At the same time, tighter capital market rules prevent the burning of excess savings, thereby increasing the risk of a crisis. In this respect too, the foundations must first be laid (by siphoning off excess savings) to ensure that stricter capital market regulations do not widen the economic demand gap.

As we have seen, the insolvency of states depends not upon whether and to what extent their government bonds have a materiel value and/or whether a country can afford to pay back debts when they become due, but solely upon whether creditors themselves are willing to prolong the debts when they fall due by issuing new loans.

A further responsibility has also fallen to the larger central banks, such as the Fed in the USA and the European Central Bank, to prevent state bankruptcies brought about by speculation on excessive debt. When powerful central banks declare that if necessary they will buy up all the distressed securities of the states in question, the securities are no longer distressed. In summer 2012 when the president of the European Central Bank, Mario Draghi, made such a declaration, the Merkel government was pleased on the one hand that a Eurozone crisis could be averted, but outraged on the other because this sort of declaration was not compatible with its guiding principles of economic policy. Again, this shows how powerless the Merkel government is to meet the economic policy challenges of our time.

Conclusion

A spectre is haunting Europe - the spectre of secular stagnation. May the politicians recognise this spectre and take off their supply-oriented blinkers! For the economic problem in secular stagnation is not a shortage of supply but a shortage of demand.

The main cause of secular stagnation is not managerial mistakes, bureaucratic obstacles or deregulated banking (although they can of course contribute to it) but the fact that purchasing power is so unequally distributed, that consumption is stagnating and that not enough can be spent on the optimal fulfilment of collective needs. The consequence is a lack of incentives to invest enough in the real economy to offset global economic savings.

This causes economic development to stagnate; the benefits of growth may be felt only by so-called 'top performers', i.e. holders of capital, managers and the most highly skilled specialists. The rest of the workforce is either made unemployed or slips into precarious work, and must be subsidised by higher earners via higher taxes and spending. Because supply-oriented economic ideology does not recognise that rising social spending is also a consequence of the unequal distribution of income and wealth, it recommends cuts to social spending in order to stimulate the economy, but this only widens the demand gap still further, and exacerbates secular stagnation.

Neoclassical economists accordingly demand that struggling European countries cut their state spending in order to reduce their debts, and are then powerless to stem the tide of falling economic demand and rising unemployment and social hardship, as well as the fact that these things are accompanied by falling tax revenues. This means that not even the goal of debt reduction is achieved.

There is a great deal of mismanagement in the struggling Eurozone countries, of course, and this must be tackled. But the only way to go about this is to redirect the public expenditure that is saved by tackling mismanagement into other forms of public spending, so as to ensure that economic demand does not collapse.

Where the deficits in public budgets and debt reduction are concerned, revenues must be increased through taxes and levies on the wealthy and those in the top income brackets, who would otherwise invest their money speculatively and even, for the most part, in other countries. The rich need to pay for debt reduction in any case, because the poor, who do not pay any taxes, do not have any money to put towards debt repayment. In other words, if we do not want economic demand to fall even further then debt reduction has to be financed by those who are also governments' creditors.

Naturally, the economically fragile countries cannot increase taxes and levies on their own, and definitely cannot raise them above the level of taxes in other countries, because then the evasive action of those affected by higher taxes and levies would do more harm than good. Only if the stronger industrialised nations set a good example, and work to combat tax avoidance strategies through international agreements, will the countries with weaker economies start asking for more money from those in their country who are rich or in possession of assets. Only then will it be fair to demand that they make higher earners pay for defaults in times of crisis instead of relying on 'bailout funds' and the acquisition of government bonds by central banks (which means the burden has to be borne by the whole Community)..

The more important a national economy is, the greater not only its influence *on* but also its responsibility *for* the global economy and/or the countries that most depend on it. Germany is the biggest economic power in Europe. Consequently, Germany carries the greatest responsibility for economic development in Europe.

The Merkel government was right to make European countries commit to not taking on any new debt. In addition to the fact that this principle is becoming more and more difficult to act upon in light of the weakness of economic demand, and because the fragile state of the global economy means new crises could break out at any time, taking an even heavier toll on public budgets, massive reductions in the debt burden are needed in the short-term in order to ward off crises resulting from the impending insolvency of individual countries

The Merkel government, however, does not recognise that debts cannot be capped and reduced by bringing in general spending cuts but only by raising taxes on higher earners and levies on wealth. Public spending on infrastructure, education, research and development, family support, the transition to renewable energy sources and a commitment to healthcare provision and old age pensions should be increased in order to combat secular stagnation. Germany should lead the way in taking this action, and act as a role model for the rest of Europe. By increasing its domestic spending Germany could also encourage imports and thus help to eliminate its chronic export and capital export surpluses.

If Germany does not do this - if it continues to implement its current supply-side economic policies - it will continue to encourage secular stagnation and increase the risk of new economic crises But in that case the Merkel government should not block the European Central Bank, even though its money gluts and low interest rate policy are contributing to the disintegration of the economy, as in so doing the ECB is, in line with the policy of *encouraging economic bubbles* as recommended by Larry Summers, promoting speculation and thus the burning of capital. If the ECB is willing even to buy government bonds of weak countries it can also prevent the risk of speculation against individual countries.

As economic difficulties intensify, however, other countries are becoming less and less willing to submit to the dictates of the Merkel government. There is thus a danger that Germany will lose its economic authority and that chaotic developments will threaten the Eurozone and ultimately also Europe.

Bibliography

Bach, Stefan u.a.: *Deutschland muss mehr in seine Zukunft investieren*, in: DIW Wochenbericht Nr. 26.2013, S.3.

BARROSO, José Manuel, *President of the EC, Statement on the TTIP*: You Tube

Bienzeisler, Bernd: *Rationalisierung im Dienstleistungssektor – Strategien und Probleme*, http://nbn-resolving.de/urn:nbn:de:0168-ssoar-116221

Shinyo Takahiro, Botschafter von Japan in Deutschland: *Die Internationale Finanz- und Wirtschaftskrise: Japans Beitrag zumKrisenmanagement.* http://www.jdzb.de/veranstaltungen/detail/?tx_ttnews[tt_news]=645&cHash=a8fbb3228137e6599895167280517ed5

Brönstrup, Carsten fragt George Soros: *„Europa droht eine lange Phase der Stagnation"* www.tagesspiegel.de/...george-soros-europa-droht-eine-lange-p...

Brönstrup, Carsten : *Der Kapitalismus nützt nur den Wohlhabenden, sagt der Ökonom Thomas Piketty. Nur mit höheren Steuern lässt sich das System retten*, in: DER TAGESSPIEGEL NR. 22 048 / 18. 5. 2014, S.22.

Brüggemeier, Franz-Josef: *Geschichte Grossbritanniens im 20. Jahrhundert*, Verlag C.H. Beck, München 2010.

Castañeda, Jorge G.: *NAFTA's Mixed Record, The View From Mexico*, published by the Council of Foreign Affairs, From our January/February 2014 Issue,
http://www.foreignaffairs.com/articles/140351/jorge-g-castaneda/naftas-mixed-record.

Colin *Clark*: *The Conditions of Economic Progress.* Macmillan, London 1940.

Das Weiße Pferd, Ausgabe 14/98: Wirtschaftskrise in Japan, *"Die wirkliche Krise kommt noch"*, www.das-weisse-pferd.com/98_14/japan.html

DIE WELT 23.12.2013: *Die großen Verlierer der Freihandelszone Nafta*, http://www.welt.de/wirtschaft/article123252705/Die-grossen-Verlierer-der-Freihandelszone-Nafta.html

DIW Pressemitteilung vom 19.03.2014: *Deflationsgefahr im Euroraum.*

dpa Basel: *100 Billionen Dollar Schulden Weltweit enormer Anstieg seit der Lehman-Pleite*, in: WWW.TAGESSPIEGEL.DE/WIRTSCHAFT, MONTAG, 10. MÄRZ 2014 / NR. 21 982, S.13.

Elsener, Dirk: *Wie die neue EZB-Politik Schattenbanken fördert*, in: THE WALL STREET JOURNALL vom 20.6.2014

Felbermayr, Gabriel, Benedikt Heid, Sybille Lehwald: *Die Transatlantische Handels- und Investitionspartnerschaft (THIP), Wem nutzt ein transatlantisches Freihandelsabkommen? Teil 1: Makroökonomische Effekte.*
http://www.bertelsmann-stiftung.de/cps/rde/xbcr/SID-291D5EE2-ADC6157/bst/xcms_bst_dms_38052_38053_2.pdf

Fratzscher, Marcel: *Die Deutschland-Illusion*, Hanser Verlag München

Fourastié, Jean 1954: *Die große Hoffnung des zwanzigsten Jahrhunderts.*

Frick, Joachim R. und Markus M. Grabka: *Gestiegene Vermögensungleichheit in Deutschland* (PDF; 276 kB). In: Wochenbericht des DIW Berlin Nr. 4/2009.

Germany Trade & Invest: *Wirtschaftsentwicklung Japan 2007*, 27.05.2008.

Hank, Rainer: *Der amerikanische Virus*, Karl Blessing Verlag 2009,

Harris, Luke Dale: *Bauernlegen auf Europäisch. Rumänien Die traditionelle Landwirtschaft hat ausgedient. Sie wird durch ein ausuferndes Land Grabbing überrollt* in: der Freitag, Nr. 19 vom 8. Mai 2014, S. 8.

Häußermann, Hartmut / Siebel, Walter 1995: *Dienstleistungsgesellschaften*, Suhrkamp *1995.*

Herbert, Ulrich über Andreas Wirsching *Das neue Europa entsteht im Geist des Neoliberalismus* in: Süddeutsche Zeitung, 13.03.2012, S.2. http://herbert.geschichte.uni- freiburg.de/herbert/beitraege/2012/Wirsching-%20Preis%20der%20Freiheit-%20SZ%2012.3.2012.pdf

Höhler, Gerd und Christopher Ziedler: *Wacklige Angelegenheit. Griechenland vermeldet erstmals seit vielen Jahren wieder einen Einnahmenüberschuss – doch Zinsen sind dabei herausgerechnet. Ist die Euro-Krise überstanden ?*in: DER TAGESSPIEGEL Nr.22025 vom 24.4.2014, S.2.

Jahnke, Joachim: *Falsch globalisiert.*
http://www.jjahnke.net/us.html
Jarecki, Eugene: *Ronald Reagan - Geliebt und gehasst,* Dokumentation http://www.politikforen.net/showthread.php?126659-Ronald-Reagan-Geliebt-und-Gehasst
Jungholt, Thorsten, Clemens Wergin: *Sicherheitskonferenz: USA und EU forcieren gigantische Freihandelszone,* Die Welt, 2. Februar 2013
Singer, K.: *Blasen her!*
http://www.timepatternanalysis.de/Blog/2013/11/27/blasen-her/
Singer, K.: Summers: *Säkulare Stagnation,*
http://www.timepatternanalysis.de/Blog/2013/11/21/summers-sakulare-stagnation/
Krugmann, Paul: *Secular Stagnation, Coalmines, Bubbles, and Larry Summers,* in New York Times November 16, 2013.
Miegel, Meinhard, Stefanie Wahl, Martin Schulte: Die Einkommensentwicklung ausgewählter Bevölkerungsgruppen in Deutschland. IWG Bonn 2008.
Neuhaus, Carla: *Die Leere der Ökonomie. Professoren ignorieren bei der Ausbildung die Finanzkrise noch immer. Studenten protestieren – und unterrichten sich selbst,* in: Der Tagesspiegel Nr. 21 918 v. 5.1.2014, S. 21.
Oswald Andreas: *Die Mittelschicht verliert Alarmierende neue Zahlen: In den USA und in Deutschland bleibt sie vom Wachstum ausgeschlossen,* in: DER TAGESSPIEGEL Nr.22025 vom 24.4.2014, S.24.
Petersen, Uwe: *Arbeitslosigkeit unser Schicksal? Wirtschaftspolitik in der Stagflation,* Verlag Peter Lang Frankfurt am Main Bern New York 1985.
same.: *Wirtschaftsethik und Wirtschaftspolitik. Zur Überwindung der globalen Wirtschaftskrise. Von der liberalen zur sozialliberalen Wirtschaftsordnung,* Verlag Dr. Kovac Hamburg 2010.
same: *Unkonventionelle Betrachtungsweisen zur Wirtschaftskrise. Von Haien, Heuschrecken und anderem Getier(I).* Verlag Peter Lang 2011.
same.: *Unkonventionelle Betrachtungsweisen zur Wirtschaftskrise II. Krankheiten des Wirtschaftssystems und Möglichkei-*

ten und Grenzen ihrer Heilung, Verlag Peter Lang 2011.
ders.: *Unkonventionelle Betrachtungsweisen zur Wirtschaftskrise III. Was ist zur Lösung der Krise zu tun?*. Verlag Peter Lang 2012, ins Englische 2013 übersetzt: *Unconventional Consideration Manners III. What is to be done for the crisis?*
Piketty, Thomas: *Das Kapital im 21. Jahrhundert*, C.H.BECK 2014.
Pilz, Gerald: *Ungewöhnliche Wertanlagen 25 Alternativen zu Festgeld & Co.*, UVK, Konstanz 2014.
Prognos AG im Auftrag der Bertelsmann Stiftung Studie: *Industrienationen profitieren von der Globalisierung weitaus stärker als Schwellen- und Entwicklungsländer* Pressemeldung Gütersloh, 24.03.2014, http://www.bertelsmann-stiftung.de/cps/rde/xchg/bst/ hs.xsl/nachrichten_120603.htm.
Reaganomics - kein Vorbild, http://www.spiegel.de/spiegel/print/d-14348704. html.
Reiermann, Christian und Anne Seith: *Währungen Die letzte Waffe*, in: Der Spiegel Nr.17/19.4.14, S. 60.
Rohleder, Christoph: *Globalisierung, Tertiarisierung und multinationale Unternehmen - Eine international vergleichende Analyse zur Diskordanz von wirtschaftlicher und politischer Entwicklung-*, Kölner Dissertation 2004.
Schratzenstaller, Margit: *Für einen produktiven und solide finanzierten Staat Determinanten der Entwicklung der Abgaben in Deutschland*, Studie im Auftrag der Abteilung Wirtschafts- und Sozialpolitik der Friedrich-Ebert-Stiftung, in: WISO Diskurs Januar 1913.
Seidel, B. 2001: *Die Einkommensteuerreform*, in: Truger, A. (Hrsg.): Rot-grüne Steuerreformen in Deutschland. Eine Zwischenbilanz, Marburg, S. 21- 46.
Singer, K.: *Summers: Säkulare Stagnation von Martin Wolf vertreten in der FT unter der Überschrift "Why the future looks sluggish".* http://www.timepatternanalysis.de/Blog/2013/11/21/summers-sakulare-stagnation.
Soros, George: *Das Krisenmanagement Angela Merkels und das mögliche Scheitern der Europäischen Union*, in: Der Tagespiegel Nr. 21970, vom 26.2.2014, S.12.

Welter, Patrick: *Thomas Piketty Ein Rockstar-Ökonom erobert Amerika*, in: FAZ Wirtschaft, http://www.faz.net/aktuell/wirtschaft/menschen-wirtschaft/thomas-piketty-ein-rockstar-oekonom-erobert-amerika-12931937.html

Willke, Gerhard: *John Maynard Keynes: Eine Einführung*, Campus Verlag Frankfurt/M. – New York 2002.

Wohltmann, Hans-Werner: *Säkulare Stagnation*, in: Gabler Wirtschaftslexikon, *http://wirtschaftslexikon.gabler.de/Definition/saekulare-stagnation.html*

Zimmermann, Elisabeth: *Siemens verschärft Arbeitsplatzabbau*, in: https://www.wsws.org/de/articles/2013/10/08/siem-o08.html

Zohlnhöfer, Werner und Reimut Zohlnhöfer: *Die Wirtschaftspolitik der Ära Kohl 1982–1989/90*. http://www.kas.de/upload/ACDP/HPM/HPM_08_01/HPM_08_01_10.pdf

Zschäpitz, Holger, Davos: *Deflationsgefahr. Geldhistoriker warnt vor fataler Abwärtsspirale* DIE WELT 24.01.14, http://www.welt.de/finanzen/article124170432/Geldhistoriker-warnt-vor-fataler-Abwaertsspirale.html

Author

Uwe Petersen born August 2.1932 in Rendsburg Germany, 1956 Diploma in Economics in Heidelberg, 1964 Doctor of Philosophy in Heidelberg (supervisor Hans-Georg Gadamer, co-supervisor Jürgen Habermas) with the thesis "The Relation of Theory and Practise in the Transcendental Phenomenology of Edmund Husserl". From 1965 in different economic groups and in the economic promotion and strategical management consultancy. Since 1998 he deals mainly with philosophy of action.

Previous Publications

Das Verhältnis von Theorie und Praxis in der Transzendentalen Phänomenologie Edmund Husserls, Dissertation Heidelberg 1964

Ost-West-Kooperation- Möglichkeiten und Grenzen, Rissener Studien, Eigenverlag HAUS RISSEN, Institut für Politik und Wirtschaft 1974

Arbeitslosigkeit unser Schicksal - Wirtschaftspolitik in der Stagflation
Peter Lang Verlag, Frankfurt/M. 1985

Finanzmittelplanung in: "Unternehmensgründung, Handbuch des Gründungsmanagements", Verlag Franz Vahlen, München 1990

Finanzmittelplanung, in "Gründungsplanung und Gründungsfinanzierung", Beck-Wirtschaftsberater im dtv, 1991,
2. völlig überarbeitete Auflage 1995, Finanzbedarfs- und Finanzierungsplanung in 3. Auflage 2000.

Das Böse in uns. Phänomenologie und Genealogie des Bösen
novum Verlag Horitschon-Wien-München 2005.

The Evil in us Phenomenology an Genealogy of Evil, novum pro Verlag 2014

Raum, Zeit, Fortschritt. Kategorien des Handelns und der Globalisierung novum Verlag, Horitschon-Wien-München 2006.

Das Verhältnis von Theorie und Praxis in der Transzendentalen Phänomenologie Edmund Husserls, Neudruck der Heidelberger Dissertation mit einem Nachtrag: *Husserl als Handlungsphilosoph*, Philosophische Reihe
Hg. J. Heil, Turnshare Ltd. London 2007.

Kreativität und Willensfreiheit im Zwielicht sinnlicher Erfahrung und theoretische Leugnung, Königshausen& Neumann, Würzburg 2007.

Religionsphilosophie der Naturwissenschaften, Philosophische Reihe
Hg. J. Heil, Turnshare Ltd. London 2007.

Sprache als wissenschaftlicher Gegenstand, philosophisches Phänomen und Tat, Königshausen& Neumann, Würzburg 2008.

Philosophie der Psychologie, Psychogenealogie und Psychotherapie.
Ein Leitfaden für Philosophische Praxis, Verlag Dr. Kovač 2010

Wirtschaftsethik und Wirtschaftspolitik. Zur Lösung der globalen Wirtschaftskrise. Von der liberalen zur sozialliberalen Wirtschaftsordnung,
Verlag Dr. Kovač 2010

Anthropologie und Handlungsphilosophie, Verlag Dr. Kovač 2011

Unkonventionelle Betrachtungsweisen zur Wirtschaftskrise. Von Haien, Heuschrecken und anderem Getier, Peter Lang Verlag 2011

Unkonventionelle Betrachtungsweisen zur Wirtschaftskrise II. Krankheiten des Wirtschaftssystems und Möglichkeiten und Grenzen ihrer Heilung. Peter Lang Verlag 2011

Unkonventionelle Betrachtungsweisen zur Wirtschaftskrise III. Was ist zur Lösung der Krise zu tun? Peter Lang Verlag 2012

Unconventional Consideration Manners of the Economic Crisis III.
What is to be done for the solution of the crisis? Peter Lang Verlag 2013

Im Anfang war die Tat I. Die Geburt des Willens in der Europäischen Philosophie
Im Anfang war die Tat II. Vom Willen zur Tat
Verlag Dr. Kovač 2012

www.ingramcontent.com/pod-product-compliance
Lightning Source LLC
Chambersburg PA
CBHW051659170526
45167CB00002B/469